W9-BUI-095

Designing Programs for
Com~~munity Grou~~

22,161

LB
2328   Designing programs for
.D4   community groups
1984

DATE DUE

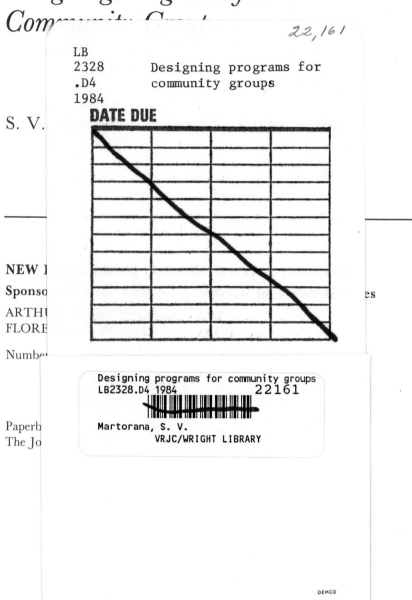

Designing programs for community groups
LB2328.D4 1984   22161

Martorana, S. V.
         VRJC/WRIGHT LIBRARY

DEMCO

S. V.

NEW

Spons   es

ARTH
FLORE

Numbe

Paperb
The Jo

Jossey-Bass Inc., Publishers
San Francisco • Washington • London

S. V. Martorana, William E. Piland (Eds.).
Designing Programs for Community Colleges.
New Directions for Community Colleges, no. 45.
Volume XII, number 1.
San Francisco: Jossey-Bass, 1983.

New Directions for Community Colleges Series
Arthur M. Cohen, *Editor-in-Chief*; Florence B. Brawer, *Associate Editor*

New Directions for Community Colleges (publication number USPS 121-710)
is published quarterly by Jossey-Bass Inc., Publishers, in association with
the ERIC Clearinghouse for Junior Colleges. *New Directions* is numbered
sequentially—please order extra copies by sequential number. The volume
and issue numbers above are included for the convenience of libraries.
Second-class postage rates paid at San Francisco, California, and at additional
mailing offices.

The material in this publication was prepared pursuant to a contract
with the National Institute of Education, U.S. Department of Education.
Contractors undertaking such projects under government sponsorship
are encouraged to express freely their judgment in professional and
technical matters. Prior to publication, the manuscript was submitted
to the Center for the Study of Community Colleges for critical review and
determination of professional competence. This publication has met such
standards. Points of view or opinions, however, do not necessarily represent
the official view or opinions of the Center for the Study of Community
Colleges or the National Institute of Education.

Correspondence:
Subscriptions, single-issue orders, change of address notices, undelivered
copies, and other correspondence should be sent to Subscriptions,
Jossey-Bass Inc., Publishers, 433 California Street, San Francisco
California 94104.

Editorial correspondence should be sent to the Editor-in-Chief,
Arthur M. Cohen, at the ERIC Clearinghouse for Junior Colleges,
University of California, Los Angeles, California 90024.

Library of Congress Catalogue Card Number LC 83-82719

International Standard Serial Number ISSN 0194-3081

International Standard Book Number ISBN 87589-987-0

Cover art by Willi Baum
Manufactured in the United States of America

This publication was prepared with funding from the National Institute of
Education, U.S. Department of Education, under contract no. 400-83-0030.
The opinions expressed in the report do not necessarily reflect the posi-
tions or policies of NIE or the Department.

Ordering Information

The paperback sourcebooks listed below are published quarterly and can be ordered either by subscription or single-copy.

Subscriptions cost $35.00 per year for institutions, agencies, and libraries. Individuals can subscribe at the special rate of $25.00 per year *if payment is by personal check.* (Note that the full rate of $35.00 applies if payment is by institutional check, even if the subscription is designated for an individual.) Standing orders are accepted. Subscriptions normally begin with the first of the four sourcebooks in the current publication year of the series. When ordering, please indicate if you prefer your subscription to begin with the first issue of the *coming* year.

Single copies are available at $8.95 when payment accompanies order, and *all single-copy orders under $25.00 must include payment.* (California, New Jersey, New York, and Washington, D.C., residents please include appropriate sales tax.) For billed orders, cost per copy is $8.95 plus postage and handling. (Prices subject to change without notice.)

Bulk orders (ten or more copies) of any individual sourcebook are available at the following discounted prices: 10–49 copies, $8.05 each; 50–100 copies, $7.15 each; over 100 copies, *inquire.* Sales tax and postage and handling charges apply as for single copy orders.

To ensure correct and prompt delivery, all orders must give either the *name of an individual* or an *official purchase order number.* Please submit your order as follows:

Subscriptions: specify series and year subscription is to begin.
Single Copies: specify sourcebook code (such as, CC8) and first two words of title.

Mail orders for United States and Possessions, Latin America, Canada, Japan, Australia, and New Zealand to:
Jossey-Bass Inc., Publishers
433 California Street
San Francisco, California 94104

Mail orders for all other parts of the world to:
Jossey-Bass Limited
28 Banner Street
London EC1Y 8QE

New Directions for Community Colleges Series
Arthur M. Cohen, *Editor-in-Chief*
Florence B. Brawer, *Associate Editor*

Contents

Editors' Notes

Among the leaders of the community college movement today, there is a sense of unease, of an unsettled condition: There is the feeling of a lost mission and of the need to recover it. This concern about the mission of community colleges is expressed in the deliberations of the board of directors and staff of the American Association of Community and Junior Colleges (AACJC); it is evident in the formal convocations of presidents and trustees of community and junior colleges (and of other community-based institutions); and it is found in the recent writings of authorities (both those who base their writings on their experiences within the movement and those who look at its progress from the outside).

Initially, when junior and, later, community colleges were making the case for and implementing the idea of educational opportunity beyond high school for all, the sense of mission was expressed and felt intensely among the presidents, trustees, scholar-researchers, and writers who were the leaders of the movement. In fact, so much was this so that observers sometimes characterized the actions of community college leadership as possessing more missionary zeal than educational substance and justification.

Still, changes in the American educational scene have occurred in large measure as a result of this sense of purpose among community colleges from the early 1900s through the present. Opportunity for all beyond the high school level is now, indeed, the rule throughout the land. Other institutions have joined in making the dream come true and extending it to even higher levels, but the community colleges showed the way.

Currently, a different concept shows promise of becoming the guiding purpose of community colleges and of other educational institutions that are deeply rooted in the localities that these institutions exist to serve. This concept is the idea that education can serve not only the interests of individual learners and of the broader, collective society but also the specialized interests of organized community groups that exist between those extremes. In every American community in which a community college is based, there typically exists a multiplicity of organizations, each with a set of wishes and characteristics different from the others that exist close by and with which each must coexist. These organizations are the focus of the new sense of mission.

1

How community colleges can further shape this new concept of their educational purpose is the main theme of this volume. This book is admittedly incomplete in its treatment of the subject, but the depth of insight shown by the authors of the eight chapters that follow and the case they make for carrying an examination of the theme much beyond this volume shout for publication and further notice.

Several of the eight chapters were originally prepared for presentation at a conference at Pennsylvania State University for persons interested and engaged in community-based postsecondary education. Other chapters were developed with this volume in mind. The structure of the volume follows the plan of the conference and begins with Eskow's statement that heretofore useful methods of building curricula and determining approaches to instruction are now outdated. No longer is it sufficient to concentrate only on the needs of individual students, on the one hand, and on those of the larger society, on the other. Needed, he suggests, is a new approach that recognizes the community as a center for the existence and operation of a host of intermediate groups — ethnic, social, cultural, political, and many others oriented differently in their purposes and their views. These, he says, can and must become a new clientele for community-based postsecondary education, for their organized needs and interests — while they are not individual, global, or even regional or national in their reach — have legitimate educational demands to be met by those who claim to want to provide educational services to all.

In subsequent chapters, each of the authors builds on the notion of the community as a center of organized special interests. Willett provides a methodology for initiating collaborative processes with organized special-interest groups in the community. Hyland probes more specifically into the existence and character of special-interest groups as consumers of postsecondary and adult education. Borgen and Shade discuss economic development as a means of serving the needs of special-interest groups, and a case study is presented suggesting that the economic development process has particular implications for the expansion and vitalization of cooperative education programs.

In Chapter Five, Goldberg discusses the need for remembering that communities have both official and unofficial groups within them that stem from state and federal interests. Then Moore presents a design for using larger normative surveys for getting initial insights into both the presence of local community groups and their major interests. The final two chapters provide (1) the observations of the editors as to the pitfalls as well as the promises associated with cooperative education and (2) a summary of the literature currently available on this topic.

All of the authors presented here agree, however, that community college programming to meet the needs of organized community groups, *as organizations,* is an idea whose time is at hand. This volume is dedicated to making it happen sooner.

S. V. Martorana
William E. Piland
Editors

S. V. Martorana is a professor in the College of Education and a research associate at the Center for the Study of Higher Education at Pennsylvania State University.

William E. Piland is professor of education at Illinois State University.

Changes in society call for an entirely new organizing principle in education that would tie the community college to associations of adult men and women.

The New Community College and the Search for Community

Seymour Eskow

A young couple wanting a good life for themselves and their children choose a community and a neighborhood and build a house. As the years go on, the neighborhood changes, the children no longer go to the neighborhood school, the children leave home, the husband changes jobs, the wife begins to work, both begin to think of retirement. Now they talk often of the neighborhood, of whether they should remain there or leave the house, with all the pull of its history, a house that has done its work well. The house, they decide meets some of their needs, particularly those of maintaining links with the past, providing the psychic support that comes from roots and memory—but it no longer offers the shelter and the way of life suited to their lives now.

My parable, of course, is meant to suggest that we look at the colleges we have built over the years, at those who now come to them, and at the neighborhoods we now have to see if they work together as well as they should. It may be that we still find that those colleges, which we have built so lovingly and which have served so many so well for so many years, no longer fit the altered conditions of community life.

The genius of the community college is its commitment to enlisting learning in the service of the local community, its harnessing

S. V. Martorana, W. E. Piland (Eds.). *Designing Programs for Community Groups.*
New Directions for Community Colleges, no. 45. San Francisco: Jossey-Bass, March 1984.

of knowledge to the cultivation of a particular landscape, culture, and people. Since all of our communities are part of a modern society under unceasing pressure from the forces of science and technology, the landscape, culture, and people change almost as we pour the footings for the new buildings on campus. Yet, in spite of these changes, the forms of the college and the community can go on serving each other, perhaps even for a long time. At some point, however, too much history and too much change have occurred for good-natured accommodation. I think that now the time has come when we must think of seriously remodeling the community college of today—not with new cosmetic facing, or trendy furniture, or additional rooms, but with fundamental redesign and rebuilding; we have to invent the new community college.

Return for a moment to the family home of our parable. Even an amateur anthropologist studying the size and arrangement of the house, examining its lot and neighborhood, and reviewing the history of demographic and physical changes in the neighborhood might make quite accurate deductions about the motives of the owners and the meaning of the house to those who lived in it. He or she might conclude without interviewing anyone that the house was built to house a large family rather than two people and that an elderly couple on a fixed income might find the maintenance and support of such a house burdensome.

What might this anthropologist learn about our colleges by studying our buildings and budgets, reading our catalogues, and looking at our students?

After looking at the size and location of our landholdings; the number and design of the buildings we place on the land; the size, use, and organization of the teaching force; the organization of curricula and the styles of pedagogy; and the nature of the auxiliary and supporting services, the anthropologist might conclude that these institutions were designed to be schools for adolescents—colleges modeled, consciously or no, on those great exemplars, the liberal arts colleges and universities. Many of our community colleges, he or she would find, have aspired to parallel the university, and, in departmental structure and style of work, they have shaped themselves in that image. The constituents of community colleges, one would conclude, were intended to be young; they would attend this total environment full time; the learning environment was designed to isolate or shield them from the workaday rhythms and concerns of the community life. Since adolescents are not yet workers, not yet parents, not yet citizens, the courses and curricula were designed to equip them to play these roles after they left. While all of the publications of the college spoke of lifelong learning, most of the formal programs of the colleges were required by law to end at the second year, so that lifelong students in search of the bachelor's degree were often forced to leave the community to achieve one — or to forgo that possibility if leaving was not practical.

The key point here is that the organizing principle of today's community college is that it is a place designed to house, teach, counsel, and serve the young. This thesis is unaffected by the older students in our classrooms or by our divisions and programs of adult education, continuing education, community service, outreach, and the like, all of which are additions and extensions of the college that do not change at all the essential shape and direction of the institution.

Suppose we could begin all over again. Suppose we were not pressured by tradition or rhetoric or external agencies to repeat the forms of the past. How would we now go about inventing and building a new college for all the community, a college of lifelong learning?

Would we use the same planning methodologies that we used originally? If we did, would we reinvent today's college with small variations? If, for example, we studied the migration of high school graduating classes, if we administered preference surveys in the high schools, if we analyzed the job market and asked employers to predict their job opportunities in the years ahead, what new results might come out of such studies? Perhaps the employers would be more interested in word processing than in secretarial science — perhaps not. The odds are great that we would be thinking about data processing and computers, large and small, but it is probable that the college of today, with minor alterations, could accommodate what the employers need. We have looked at our communities in traditional ways that may no longer suffice. If we continue to look in those ways, we will reinvent the same types of colleges, which is not our goal.

Kenneth Burke has reminded us that the ways in which we have seen our communities have also been ways of not seeing our communities. If we want to change our field of vision in order to see new possibilities, we have to change the lenses through which we look and use lenses of wider angle that take in more than the youth culture has shown to us by the lenses of the past. Young people and their search for identity, competence, and career will continue to engage much of our attention; we now have to see with equal clarity all of the other publics of our community.

I propose that a new sociology and a new psychology can help us see our communities in ways that will allow us to create new institutional forms, curricula, and strategies of teaching and learning to serve what we see.

Associations: The Community College
and the American Community

This sociology is new only in that we of the colleges have not customarily applied it to our studies of our communities. The perspective and the methodology themselves are quite old; they go back to 1835, when a thirty-year-old French aristocrat, Alexis de Tocqueville, published the first volume of his great *Democracy in America.*

De Tocqueville (1959 [1840], p. 117) found one of the keys to American democracy and community strength in what he called *association*: "Feelings and opinions are recruited, the heart is enlarged, and the human mind is developed only by the reciprocal influence of men upon each other. I have shown that these influences are almost entirely null in democratic countries; they must therefore be artificially created, and this can only be accomplished by association." In America, according to de Tocqueville (1959 [1840], p. 114), associations have become the engines of local and national progress:

> Americans of all ages, all conditions, and all dispositions constantly form associations. They have not only commercial and manufacturing companies in which they all take part, but associations of a thousand other kinds — religious, moral, serious, futile, general or restricted, enormous or diminutive. The American makes associations to give entertainments, to found seminaries, to build inns, to construct churches, to diffuse books, to send missionaires to antipodes: They found in this manner hospitals, prisons, and schools. If it be proposed to inculcate some truth, or to foster some feeling by the encouragement of a great example, they form a society. Wherever, at the head of some new undertaking, you see the government in France, or a man of rank in England, in the United States you will be sure to find an association.

This view of the nature of American society, in other hands and eyes, became the stuff of satire, describing Americans as mindless joiners, organization men, Babbitts. But to de Tocqueville, individualism, which dissolved the social nexus and taught people to value private pursuits over the common good, was the greater threat. "If men are to remain civilized, or to become so," he wrote, "the art of associating together must grow and improve in the same ratio in which the equality of conditions is increased" (p. 118). Political associations, he said, are the "large free schools, where all the members of the community go to learn the general theory of association" (p. 125).

When we look at our communities through the lens of de Tocqueville's theory of associations, we no longer see disconnected human atoms to be polled, assessed, brought to campus for instruction, and discharged as educated. We see rather a rich, dense fabric of group life, much of it rooted in place and culture, all of it representing the concerns and the commitment of those who come together. If associations are the seedbed of American democracy, the "large free schools" where we go to learn the arts of conversation, the principles of sharing, and the strategies of democracy, the question now arises: What is the obligation of the community college to these groups?

Suppose we inventory and classify the associations of our community. We find groups that are functions of *place* — neighborhoods with structures and styles that are distinct, often representing a unique heritage or subculture. We find *ethnic and religious groups* — Protestants, Catholics, Jews, the Ancient Order of Hibernians, the Sons of Italy, the Jewish Community Center. Some groups are *age-related* — Golden Age clubs, youth centers. Others are *economic* or *political,* and there is a rather long list of public and private associations concerned with *culture* — museums, galleries, theaters, orchestras, and the groups that voluntarily run and support them.

If the new community college were to see its role as using learning to dignify and strengthen associated life in the community, how might it set about doing this?

It might, for one, create neighborhood colleges on the model of educational settlement houses — colleges that would be of, for, and by the people of the neighborhood, reflecting in their curricula and services the neighborhood's issues and needs, so that the character and quality of each neighborhood's unit would be those of the neighborhood itself. The neighbors would, of course, be free to go to the main campus for its libraries and rich academic bill of fare, but the neighborhood college would be there to offer something other than English 101 — perhaps English as a Second Language or courses in applied sociology that allowed neighbors to examine and strengthen neighborhood institutions.

If our communities include what Michael Novak (1972) has called "unmeltable ethnics," Americans who refuse to throw their ancestral cultures and group identities into the melting pot, could our colleges take on the role of guardian of the music, art, dance, and literature of these cultures, to help keep them vital and visible? Could we (should we) organize new lower-division liberal arts curricula in Irish studies, Italian studies, Puerto Rican studies — curricula, in other words, that encourage students to learn the history, culture, and language of their own (or someone else's) ethnic or religious heritage, and that include a semester or a summer in Ireland, Italy, or Puerto Rico as a part of the program?

Similarly, should we have programs in Christian studies so that old and young can explore together their religion, its history, literature, rituals, and sociology, at college and in the community as well as at church? Or does the theory and practice of community education mean that we must keep out of the curriculum the great searchers for human meaning that are found in our religious and our racial and ethnic sub-cultures on the grounds that such curricula would lead to division and the loss of a common academic culture? If we are not to engage our citizens as Protestants, Catholics, and Jews, as Irish and Italians, then we are required to avoid these associations that engage the affections and energies of many of these citizens.

There may seem to be little point in lingering over the role of the community college in the economic realm, since we have been pledged to business and industry, to jobs and careers, since our inception. As we look closely at our ideology of career, however, and the curricula it has created, questions come quickly. Our theory commits us to preparing technicians, semiprofessionals, and paraprofessionals—what used to be called "middle-level manpower," since moving technicians further up the educational ladder is the role of the senior college and preparing students for the trades and crafts is usually the work of the secondary schools. How useful are these restraints and limits today? What, if anything, can we do about preparing people to create work rather than fill jobs? In many of our communities, there is simultaneously a shortage of jobs in existing businesses and industries and much work to be done that people will pay for but that has not yet been turned into a business. Can the community college develop entrepreneurs and help them launch small businesses? And can the community learn to work with the small businesses that now exist so that they might be helped to survive and grow, creating more jobs in the process?

Our chambers of commerce, our trade associations, and our agencies of local government are struggling with the theory and practice of economic development. The questions they are looking at are central to the economic health of each community: What businesses and industry do we now have? How well are they doing? What do they need to maintain themselves and grow? What kind of help is it possible and proper to give them? What assets do we have that might attract new businesses and new jobs to our community? How do we present ourselves effectively to businesses around the country and the world so that they might consider coming here?

What is the community college's role in the raising and the

answering of such questions? Can the community college use its talents in social science and statistics to help our economic development agencies do the research on which their plans must rest? Can our business students and faculty members learn by participating in such studies and promotional activities?

If, as de Tocqueville suggested, politics is the free school of democracy, might the community college become the large free school of politics? Can we allow and encourage our students and their teachers to engage in partisan politics without the institution itself being seen as partisan? Should there be action-oriented curricula in public service that offer students internships in practical politics at the local, state, or national levels? Our nurses learn to nurse by taking their theory to the hospital; why shouldn't students of sociology and political science test their learning in the streets, in city hall, in the state capitol?

In all of our communities, those who want to learn or to practice an art or craft can find cultural agencies that offer facilities, apprenticeship, and an association of the like-minded. Often these agencies are marginal financially, are going under, or are curtailing programs and services. Can we join with them without absorbing them, without sapping the voluntarism of their efforts, without dominating? Would they allow their theaters to act as laboratory theaters for our colleges, much as our community hospitals serve our nursing students, in a relationship that would permit us to help them in exchange for their services to us? And if we have theaters and galleries of our own, should we not assign a good portion of their use to the artists in our communities and their organizations, so that they might develop their talents through exhibition and performance while they enrich the climate of our campuses?

If we are to become new community colleges, we have to see our communities in new ways, and one such way is as an orchestra of associations. We have to meet these groups on their turf as well as ours, to exchange agendas and to search together for opportunities for mutual service.

At least three educational strategies for connecting with the associated life of our communities are possible. The first is the familar academic response of *curriculum:* We create programs in Irish studies, or Christian studies, or performing arts. The second practice is *cosponsorship:* The college and the association design and mount programs together in ways that allow both to be visible and to share credit. Another emerging practice of great promise is called *brokering:* The college sees itself at the center of a constellation of agencies, organizations, facilities, and places; it sees all of these as learning environments or community classrooms, and it links, or brokers, people wanting to learn to the appropriate community setting. At the same time, the college provides for these groups courses, conferences, workshops, and institutes, either on campus or in the community.

From a Psychology of Adolescence to a Psychology of the Adult

If the anthropologist we invoked earlier returned to study our admissions offices and practices, our student personnel services and counseling styles, our student unions and student activities, our teacher-student relations, and our grading practices, he or she might conclude that these all rest upon a "psychology of the adolescent."

The new psychology that will help us to see the changing life needs of the adults in our community is penetrating the literature, appearing on our lecture platforms, and making its way into our colleges. Perhaps the seminal figure in the movement is Erik Erikson, whose work on identity and the stages and crises of life has been moved into popular consciousness by Gail Sheehy's *Passages* (1976).

Erikson (1975) distinguishes eight stages of life. K. Patricia Cross (1981), synthesizing the work of such investigators as Sheehy, Chickering, Havighurst, and Levinson, uses seven. Table 1 shows the seven stages as described by Cross.

For each age-related stage or phase of life, there are "marker events" that symbolize, embody, and realize the "psychic tasks" that must be undertaken and accomplished so that the person can move on to the next phase of the journey. Also, for each phase there is a "characteristic stance"—that is, the perspective or the pervasive mood that animates the person.

As we look at the marker events and psychic tasks in the first phase, ages eighteen to twenty-two, and the last phase, age sixty-five and beyond, it becomes clear that the colleges do much to help the first group with its psychic tasks and rites of passage and little or nothing to help the sixty-five-year-old in the community prepare for retirement, physical decline, financial pressures, loneliness, and death.

The names and functions of key agencies in our colleges reveal our historic commitment to adolescents. We have an admissions office, and our officers talk and think a great deal about high school counselors and high school seniors. In the folders of applicants are secondary school transcripts, intelligence quotient (IQ) and other test scores, and data that have very little to do with changing one's work at fifty-five, with retirement at sixty-five, or with divorce or unemployment at any age.

Table 1. Cross's Seven Stages of Life

Phase and Age	Marker Events	Psychic Tasks	Characteristic Stance
Leaving Home 18–22	Leave home Establish new living arrangements Enter college Start first full-time job Select mate	Establish autonomy and independence from family Define identity Define sex role Establish new peer alliances	A balance between "being in" and "moving out" of the family
Moving into Adult World 23–28	Marry Establish home Become parent Get hired/fired/quit job Enter into community activities	Regard self as adult Develop capacity for intimacy Fashion initial life structure Build the dream Find a mentor	"Doing what one should" Living and building for the future Launched as an adult
Search for Stability 29–34	Establish children in school Progress in career or consider change Possible separation, divorce, remarriage Possible return to school	Reappraise relationships Reexamine life structure and present commitments Strive for success Search for stability, security, control Search for personal values Set long-range goals Accept growing children	"What is this life all about now that I am doing what I am supposed to?" Concern for order and stability and with "making it" Desire to set long-range goals and meet them
Becoming One's Own Person 37–42	Crucial promotion Break with mentor Responsibility for three-generation family—that is, for growing children and aging parents For women: empty nest; enter career and education	Face reality Confront mortality; sense of aging Prune dependent ties to boss, spouse, mentor Reassess marriage Reassess personal priorities and values	Suspended animation More nurturing stance for men; more assertive stance for women "Have I done the right thing? Is there time to change?"

Table 1. Cross's Seven Stages of Life, Cont'd.

Phase and Age	Marker Events	Psychic Tasks	Characteristic Stance
Settling Down 45–55	Cap career Become mentor Launch children; become grandparents New interests and hobbies Physical limitations; menopause Active participation in community events	Increase feelings of self-awareness and competence Reestablish family relationships Enjoy one's choices and life style Reexamine the fit between life structure and self	"It is perhaps late, but there are things I would like to do in the last half of my life." Best time of life
The Mellowing 57–64	Possible loss of mate Health problems Preparation for retirement	Accomplish goals in the time left to live Accept and adjust to aging process	Mellowing of feelings and relationships Spouse increasingly important Greater comfort with self
Life Review 65 +	Retirement Physical decline Change in finances New living arrangements Death of friends/spouse Major shift in daily routine	Search for integrity versus despair Acceptance of self Disengagement Rehearsal for death of spouse	Review of accomplishments Eagerness to share everyday human joys and sorrows Family is important Death is a new presence

Sources: Chickering and Havighurst, 1981; Gould, 1972; Lehman and Lester, 1978; Levinson and others, 1974; McCoy, Ryan, and Lictenberg, 1978; Neugarten, 1968; Sheehy, 1976; Weathersby, 1978.

Source: Cross, 1981, pp. 174–175.

We are beginning to realize that retirement is not an unskilled occupation. The observation grows in meaning as one dwells upon it; being divorced, widowed, unemployed—none of life's crises and passages are unskilled occupations. Trained and available counselors familiar with adult development problems, books, and courses can help furnish us with the skills and insights we need to cope with life's demands, and the community college might become in each community the agency that can work in this way with all adults.

One appealing notion is to replace the admissions office with a "life skills center." The life skills center would be staffed by adult counseling specialists of two kinds: Some would be expert in counseling with those of a particular age; others would be experienced in helping adults work with those crises that can afflict us at any age, such as joblessness, or bereavement, or divorce.

Our sociology of associations and our psychology of the life cycle come together. To deal with our crises, many of us need the help of our fellows, the support of other men and women who have been through what we are enduring or undertaking or who have resources of insight and training that they will share with us. In almost every American community, there are associations that can help us with our drinking, our singleness, our searches for meaningful work, for expression, or transcendence. And, often, as we find the group that is organized around a life need, we find also a small community, a community that helps us overcome the feelings of isolation, loneliness, and despair that afflict so many of us in modern America.

Shaping the New Community College

The form the new community college will take after it learns the sociology of its community, incorporates the groups it finds, and designs new instruments serving men and women of all ages is open to speculation.

The present buildings, removed as they may be from the vortex of community life, will continue to be the right learning environment for those who want to retreat from the maelstrom at times to wonder, reflect, and look quietly at their lives; for many in the community, the community college campus will continue to provide a secular monastery. The present curricular organization of small course packages— three hours a week for three credits—will continue to be useful to those adults who can only be, or want to be, part-time students, whose needs for association are met elsewhere, and who want only competence in a skill, a motive to read and reflect, or a certificate or degree.

But there are as many or more adults who would welcome the opportunity to become part of an intellectual community on campus, and the present mode of organizing the mass community college simply does not offer such a community to students in the arts and sciences. (There is often genuine community in the nursing and technology departments, on the other hand, where masters and apprentices, united in their quest for skill and service, become an association rather than simply an audience for their teachers.) The community college movement, then, must revive and take seriously the idea of the *cluster college,* the notion that the mass institution can be scaled to the size and needs of human beings by dividing it into small learning companies or colleges. Under this plan, colleges would be created around a learning style, a set of themes, a vocation, or a cause, and the teachers and students would select themselves into the colleges that interest them.

In every community there are men and women, young and old, who define themselves as writers — as poets, dramatists, novelists, journalists. Our theory and practice of curriculum allows our nursing students to join a community of nurses immediately, while our poets are counseled to take two years of general and liberal education — perhaps with a course or two in poetry — and to "major" in poetry in the senior college. Such an education thwarts the deepest needs of these students and pushes their search for identity and for mastery of their craft to the outskirts of their lives — or at least to their after-college hours. If we were to bring together our writer-teachers and our writer-students in a curriculum that makes writing the organizing center and major field of study, we should have more and better poets in our colleges and our land and more joy in learning.

Other possibilities crowd in. Why could there not be a small St. John's Community College on campus, for those who want a rigorous, prescribed, Socratic curriculum grounded on the great books? Or a Northeastern Community College for those who want to marry theory and practice, to work and study, to serve and learn? Or an International Community College, for those interested in culture, language, and overseas work and study? The promise of cluster colleges is that they would bring de Tocqueville to the campus: The community college could become a college of colleges, of associations of men and women in search of learning who also find communion and community.

The Community College and Distance Learning

The term *pedagogy* refers to the instruction of children, as pediatrics refers to their doctoring. It has been suggested that we use the new coinage *andragogy* to refer to the institution of adults. Perhaps we are uncomfortable with the word, but it makes the point: We must not assume that ways of teaching the young are necessarily apt for teaching their elders. If the community college prides itself on its single-minded devotion to teaching and if the new community college increasingly teaches adults, then the community college must become a leader in the development of the new andragogy.

Since the life needs of adults include obligations other than formal study and require their presence regularly at places far from campus, the new andragogy will have to liberate learning from the tyrannies of time and place. The campus-bound, schedule-dominated, teacher-centered pedagogies of today will have to make way for other ways of learning that can happen in other places, at other times, and with no teachers or with those who are not primarily teachers but are willing to share what they know.

Recent efforts to revive and update the old British tradition of the external degree have resulted in credit-by-examination and degree-by-examination programs that allow adult students to travel, work, or care for children while reading, writing, and preparing to demonstrate competence. The Council on Accreditation of Experiential Learning (CAEL) has developed a set of tough-minded, practical strategies for assessing learning acquired by experience, and the CAEL body of practice is available to any community college that chooses to use it.

The British Open University has sparked the development of a worldwide theory and practice of "distance learning." Distance learning uses carefully designed home study materials, augmented by well-produced radio and television programs; it uses the computer as well as tutors for the marking of papers and examinations submitted by students; and it incorporates regional centers (for those who want human tutoring) and yearly seminars to bring students together with teachers. Many adults cannot leave home easily—mothers with infants, for example, or the ill—and others are in hospitals or prisons. Unless we design programs that can be sent to the home or institution, we deny such adults the instruction and the competence they want and need. Furthermore, the newer technologies of cable television and the microcomputer suggest that we *can* use the home or institution as learning centers, with access through these and other technologies to live teachers and counselors.

Many American educators are examining the Scandinavian study circle movement as they look for styles of learning that adults find congenial. We hear that in Norway five hundred thousand people of a population of four million are enrolled in study circles. A study circle is a small group of adults—members of a social circle, a church, a union, or a work group—who choose to meet together regularly to study, to read, and to discuss. The regional study circle authority, in the Norwegian scheme, underwrites most of the cost of reading materials and of a leader, who is often not a trained teacher. The group meets regularly at the homes of members or at a convenient meeting place to talk, study, and, importantly, to socialize: Study becomes part of an adult sharing of good talk and good times, organically connected to other needs of those who want to be with each other.

While Scandinavia is receiving much attention now for its public support of the study circle idea, it should be noted that study circles have a long and unbroken history in the United States. The Chautauqua movement, under the leadership of William Rainey Harper, created a national network of literary circles toward the end of the last century, and a number of these are still in existence; the Great Books Foundation has study circles in hundreds of communities in the country; a number of churches and synagogues have elaborate machinery for the creation of materials to support study circle networks; and such groups as the League of Women Voters are sophisticated users of the study circle for their purposes. Many adults like to study this way. Can the community college become the center of the study circle movement in each community, providing training for leaders, helping to find and develop materials, attaching the study circle idea to existing groups, and creating new study circles when there is an evident need?

Perhaps the most imaginative device of the new andragogy is not the camera or the computer but the "learning contract," which borrows the ancient notion of the don or preceptor, renames him or her "mentor," and uses a written bilateral agreement between mentor and student to record the goals, learning experiences, and methods of evaluating a program of study designed by the mentor and student. The contract tells the student what he or she agrees to accomplish, what to read and write, where to work (if work is part of the agreement), and what evidence of learning—in the form of papers, records, pictures, artifacts, or studies—he or she is to transmit to the mentor for judgment and credit. Armed with such a contract, some books and papers, and perhaps some letters of introduction, the student can study at home, in a neighboring state, or make India or England the classroom. The idea of the contract acknowledges that adults can learn while not under the direct tutelage of the teacher, that the teacher can be a shaping influence even if he or she is not regularly before the student, and that the adult can learn from the places, the things, the agencies, and the cultures of the world.

When colleges believed that a map or two, some books in the library, and perhaps a chemistry laboratory were essential to higher learning, one could imagine assembling under one roof (or a series of roofs on some acres of land) all of the instruments of learning and all of the teachers one might need. Over the years, impelled by this ideal of the campus as a self-contained city of learning, we have built more buildings, created more laboratories, and purchased larger pieces of equipment, always trying to create a total environment for learning. In recent years, most of us have seen the impossibility of that dream: The latest equipment is sometimes too large, often too expensive, and is usually obsolete even as it is installed. And, more importantly, it now seems sensible to us to have adults preparing for life and career in the community, using the equipment and the environments of the community itself as their laboratories and the practitioners in those environments as their teachers. Why simulate the hospital on campus for our nursing students when there are real hospitals in the community? And why not use for other students real banks, real offices, or real computer centers? Increasingly, then, the community itself is becoming the teacher.

Conclusion

This chapter includes only one of two themes that might animate eduational discourse in the immediate future and might inform the new community colleges we shall be building. Our theme here has been that of *community* — the renewal of local community life in America and the part that education can play in that renewal. The other theme is *world* — the need to include in the agenda of every community college ways in which adults can become open to the new global order that is emerging and ways in which to prepare them for work and citizenship in that global community.

There are those who think that an education that celebrates community — the small, the local, the neighborly — will breed provincials and parochials rather than the world citizens we now need, and there are those who believe that bringing the world into the college curriculum will deracinate our students, make them aliens in their home towns, and indifferent to the claims of the community. But, as John Dewey wrote, we cannot love the neighbor we have not seen if we do not love the neighbor we see every day; that compassion, like charity, begins at home and then overflows the borders of home to embrace the strangers outside our door. The new community college will find itself inevitably becoming a world college and finally, a "world community" college.

20

References

Cross, K. P. *Adults as Learners: Increasing Participation and Facilitating Learning.* San Francisco: Jossey-Bass, 1981.

Dewey, J. *The Public and Its Problems.* Chicago: Swallow Press, 1954.

Erikson, E. H. *Life History and the Historical Moment.* New York: Norton, 1975.

Novak, M. *The Rise of the Unmeltable Ethnics.* New York: MacMillan, 1972.

Sheehy, G. *Passages: Predictable Crises of Adult Life.* New York: Dutton, 1976.

Tocqueville, A. de. *Democracy in America.* vol. 2. New York: Vantage Books, 1959 (originally published 1840).

Seymour Eskow, former president of Rockland Community College, is directing a special project of the American Association of Community and Junior Colleges called "Putting America Back to Work."

When collaborative efforts take a positive orientation toward the future from their inception, they have greater chances of success.

Initiating the College-Community Collaborative Process

Lynn H. Willett

The futurist Robert Theobald (1983) has observed that many professionals in education lack the minimum skills to initiate cooperative ventures within the community. Yet, while they lack the necessary skills, most college professionals realize that cooperative ventures with other local community agencies are a worthy goal. There seems to be a reluctance to develop skills and competencies to initiate successful college-community linkages. This reluctance stems not from a negative philosophical position but from the person's inner psychological needs for independence, control, recognition, and expedience. Here are some of the ways in which the hidden voices of college professionals might verbalize their experiences and concerns regarding cooperative agreements:

- "I usually get the short end of the stick."
- "I wasn't involved at the design stage of the cooperative process."
- "My time in the execution phase was never utilized effectively."
- "Most of the coordinating meetings were long and boring."
- "There seemed to be underlying premeeting agreements among the key collaborators."
- "The whole project seemed to be a total waste of time and energy."

S. V. Martorana, W. E. Piland (Eds.). *Designing Programs for Community Groups.*
New Directions for Community Colleges, no. 45. San Francisco: Jossey-Bass, March 1984.

- "Credit for the project's success was not given to everyone."
- "No one ever laid out beforehand all of the steps we were going to go through to achieve our goal."
- "It seemed like we were in a dark tunnel."

These are typical inner voices of resistance; their sentiments are shared by both the initial collaborators and others invited to join in later. These resistance points can be overcome if a future-based linkage process is implemented early in the collaboration. This process should be implemented prior to the traditional planning sequence of setting goals, evaluating strategy, and planning action.

The future-based strategy (Lindaman and Lippitt, 1979) provides a similar starting point for all participants and utilizes the person's internal feelings of resistance as part of the initial data base. The futuring process helps to swing the participants' focus from the past and present to the future. The central goal of the futuring strategy, in fact, is to get the collaborators to agree on a concrete image of the future cooperative venture. Once this has been accomplished the traditional planning process can begin. Figure 1 depicts the major activities in the futuring-planning process and also displays a pie diagram of the amount of time allocated to futuring and to planning.

Once the collaborators have agreed to use the future-based strategy, its participatory design process, built on sound social psychological principles (Rothman, 1974; Rothman and others, 1976) and good meeting processes (Schindler-Rainman and Lippitt, 1975), will result in a strong consensus and commitment for interagency cooperation.

The model for developing collaboration advocated in this chapter has been drawn largely from the writings and seminars of Dr. Ron Lippitt, professor emeritus at the University of Michigan. Lippitt's strategy has been distilled into a six-step model, which, if followed, will result in successful and productive linkages between community colleges and local community interest groups. The six steps in this process are: (1) recruiting the right people, (2) creating a common data base, (3) imaging a cooperative venture, (4) prioritizing, (5) integrating, and (6) planning action. It is also possible to modify steps four, five, and six to take into account goal definition and the importance of goal hiatus — that is, the gap between the aspirations and the achievement levels of current institutional goals (Martorana and Kuhns, 1975).

Recruiting the Right People

The first phase in the process centers on finding the right people through the nomination of volunteers. Too often organizations appoint

Figure 1. Pie Diagram of Linkage Process

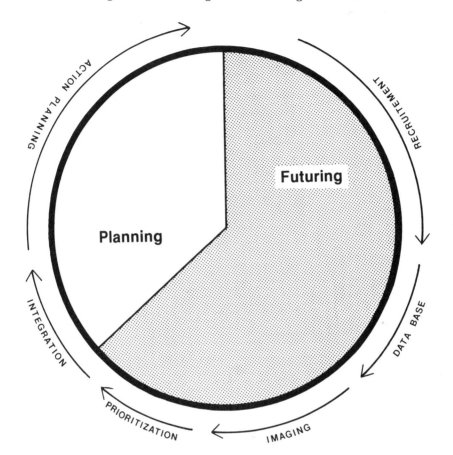

or elect people to committees, which creates the wrong state of mind for the committee member. The most important motivator in a cooperative venture is the individual's personal commitment. This personal commitment will result in the release of extraordinary creative energies throughout the entire process.

A successful strategy for finding the right people is to ask a variety of informed members of the collaborative groups to name individuals in their organization or community group who play key or influential roles. Very quickly, the initiator or facilitator of the cooperative process will find that certain individuals are mentioned or identified multiple times. Once this nominating information has been collected and presented to the potential participant, he or she is inclined to say yes and also to feel positive about participation.

The key steps in this phase of the process include the following:

1. Determine the general topic for collaboration.
2. Gather a small group to help in eliciting nominations for the collaborative process.
3. Ask various people who they think would be interested in working on the project.
4. Pool the nomination data and designate the most appropriate person to contact those nominated.
5. Initiate a general invitation for interested volunteers.
6. Call a short meeting of those committed.
7. Discuss the general design and responsibilities for the process.
8. Designate one location and one time for a collaborative forum.

Creating a Common Data Base

Once the first step is accomplished the focus of energy is on developing and executing a one-shot meeting where all participants are equally involved and share the same futuring and planning experiences. The first activity in the one-shot meeting is to develop a common data base.

There are a number of effective strategies for creating a common base among people recruited to the forum. One of the most powerful and effective strategies is to utilize the brainstorming technique. Initially, participants in the process should be asked to brainstorm about successful and unsuccessful cooperative ventures in the past in which they have been involved. These views should be posted on newsprint.

Once this retrospective brainstorming has occurred, the next step in developing a common data base is to ask these participants to identify the key events, trends, and developments (ETDs) that are currently occurring within their organization or their community group. As part of this process, participants should discuss the significant trends occurring in society as a whole. Then, by brainstorming about these data, the group can arrive at coherent statements that express the key events, trends, and developments in the special-interest organization in which the cooperative venture is to take place. These ETDs should be posted on newsprint, and all participants should read and discuss the data.

The key steps in this process, then, include the following:

1. Plan and organize the one-shot meeting.
2. Mix group members in small four- or five-member brainstorming groups.
3. Present some general events, trends, and developments occurring throughout society at this time and have the groups discuss.
4. Conduct small-group ETD brainstorming sessions.
5. Discuss and crystallize the significant ETDs from step four.
6. Post and read all ETDs.

Imaging the Cooperative Venture

The next major activity initiating an effective cooperative process is to ask the participants to visualize what might be accomplished one year hence. Then, when the participants have put themselves "into the future," they should report what pleases them about their accomplishment. This process takes the collaborators out of the present and creates a positive motivation for each of them, since they have begun to think positively and creatively about the future.

This imaging process can be accomplished either in a group brainstorming session or on an individual basis, utilizing the ETD information that was generated during the data base phase. After all of the positive aspects of the future images have been recorded on newsprint, this list should be reviewed by everybody. The next step will be to select a priority image on which the group can focus.

The key steps in this phase of the process include the following:
1. Encourage participants to see their idea as an image in the future (one year ahead).
2. Record via brainstorming the positive feelings and ideas that the participants have about their image being accomplished.
3. Encourage participants to be reality-oriented and concrete in reporting their image ideas.
4. Have everyone review all of the posted data.

Prioritizing

The group facilitator will find that a large number of creative future images were developed during the imaging phase of the process. The next important activity is to determine which of these future images are feasible and are of most interest to the participants. The prioritizing process should utilize two or three key feasibility tests that the future image must pass. In this phase, the group is working toward agreement on one or two images. For example, key feasibility test questions may concern the likelihood of successful accomplishment, the cost to implement, the probability of obtaining sanction from higher authorities, the degree of innovativeness, or the likelihood of involving other key resource people in the special-interest group to work on the particular activity.

Once there has been group agreement on two or three feasibility criteria, each member should then vote for two or three of the images that were generated in the imaging phase. This will result in a drastic shrinkage of the number of future images. At this point, the group should doublecheck the relationship of the proposed future images to the current major goals of the institution, Martorana and Kuhns (1975, 1978) suggest. Doing this increases the likelihood that actions to be decided upon later in the model's application will bear meaningfully on goals of the highest priority in the institution. The last step in the prioritization is to have the individuals vote by checking off the particular image to which they personally would like to commit time and energy to accomplish.

The key steps in this process include the following:
1. Brainstorm feasibility criteria.
2. Select two or three criteria.
3. Assess through discussion the feasibility of each image.
4. Vote on images on which participants like to work.

Integrating Images in a Scenario

After the various future images have been prioritized and agreed upon, the group needs to pull together the image fragments into coherent pictures of the future activity that will become the group's collaborative undertaking. In other words, one or two people should take the image fragments from the preceding step and write a statement of them that is concrete; this statement becomes a future scenario. The scenario should specify an outcome as well as a target date for completion. These statements then form the basis for an action plan, as Figure 1 indicates. The more specific and realistic the future scenarios, the better the planning process will be—and the greater the likelihood of accomplishing the plan.

Another alternative in the integration phase would be to write traditional goals and objectives statements. Here again, it is important to note that the level to which an institution's goals are aspired and the level to which they are achieved vary (Martorana and Kuhns, 1975); the consequent hiatus is an important factor to take into account in long-range planning. The resulting goal statements feed into the first steps in the traditional planning process.

The key steps in this phase, then, include the following:

1. Bring together the image ideas and collapse them into a limited number.
2. Designate one or two people to write a coherent statement describing the future image (or goal) with a set of features (or scenarios) describing more specific elements of the goal.

Action Planning

The final major activity is the action planning. Using the integrated statements and scenarios from the previous step, the group performs a force-field analysis. A force-field analysis (Lewin, 1947) attempts to identify the barriers and support forces that are at work in any change activity (see Figure 2 for an example). Once the force-field analysis has been brainstormed by the entire group, a discussion should be held to identify the one or two supporting forces and the one or two key restraining forces on which the group feels they can work. These key supporting and resisting forces then become the basis for specific activity planning.

Next, the group should brainstorm the first steps for dealing with these supporting and resisting forces. When joined with an analysis of hiatus between aspiration and achievement levels of current institutional goals, this brainstorming generates a very specific list of

Figure 2. Force-Field Analysis of Cooperative State Grant for Unemployed Workers

Barriers or Resistances to Activity	*Supports or Resources for Activity*
Who will administer the grant?	Funding agency favors multiparty application.
We won't agree on project procedures.	Our pooled strengths predict project effectiveness.
We may do more work than other agency.	We can divide up the work of writing grant.
Our agency has had track record with state funding agency.	We can develop political pressure to obtain funding.
Community doesn't have many new jobs.	One agency has great volunteer network.

activities that, through their accomplishment, will ensure progress toward accomplishing the future image goal outlined earlier.

At this point, task forces should be organized around key activities. These volunteer task forces must be given adequate resources and support so that they can carry out their specific plans. It is important in action planning to identify rewards for the group. Another important feature at this stage is to identify small incremental steps so that people have a feeling of progress. Also, feedback mechanisms should be indicated so that change and progress are recorded and disseminated once the activity has been initiated.

The key steps in this final phase of the process include the following:

1. Conduct a force-field brainstorming session.
2. Identify one or two key restraining and one or two key supporting forces.
3. Brainstorm key start-up activities to overcome the issues in step two.
4. Pull together this activity list and sequence in a timeline organized from the first activity possible to do to the last possible.
5. Identify appropriate rewards and feedback at various steps in the activity list from step four.
6. Conduct a great celebration for whole group because you have completed all the tasks of the collaborative forum!

Conclusion

Colleges can link successfully with local community interest groups. The model presented in this chapter rests basically on Lippitt's strategies as outlined in this six-phase collaborative process, but modifications that bring in other theoretical approaches are possible and some are suggested here. These six phases will result not only in a group feeling of ownership but also in providing an activity that is innovative and futuristic in addition to being feasible and realistic.

The tasks involved in implementing the basic model include: conducting a nomination process for participation, identifying a common setting where a cooperative meeting can occur, structuring the meeting process so it meets the criteria of a good meeting format, conducting brainstorming sessions, conducting a future-imaging process, writing future scenarios, conducting a force-field analysis, planning activities with task forces, and identifying rewards and feedback mechanisms.

References

Lewin, K. "Frontiers in Group Dynamics: Concepts, Method, and Reality in Social Science, Social Equilibrium, and Social Change." *Human Relations,* 1947, *1,* 5–41.

Lindaman, E., and Lippitt, R. *Choosing the Future You Prefer.* Bethesda, Md.: Development Publications, 1979.

Martorana, S. V., and Kuhns, E. *Managing Academic Change: Interactive Forces and Leadership in Higher Education.* San Francisco: Jossey-Bass, 1975.

Martorana, S. V., and Kuhns, E. "Analyzing a Force for Change: Discrepancy Between Aspiration and Achievement of Institutional Goals." Paper published in the proceedings of the 18th annual meeting of the Association for Institutional Research, Houston, Texas, May 1978.

Rothman, J. *Planning and Organizing for Social Change.* New York: Columbia University Press, 1974.

Rothman, J., Erlick, J., and Teresa, J. *Promoting Innovation and Change in Organizations and Communities.* New York: Wiley, 1976.

Schindler-Rainman, E., and Lippitt, R. *Taking Your Meetings out of the Doldrums.* San Diego, Calif.: University Associates, 1975.

Theobald, R. Unpublished comments presented at the World Futures Conference for Education, Dallas, Tex., 1983.

Lynn H. Willett is vice-president for Institutional and Community Development at Elgin Community College in Illinois.

*Community-related education involves colleges in the
social struggles of their constituencies, in the renegotiations
of accepted roles and practices, and it creates the setting
for challenging programs.*

Working with Communities
as Centers of
Special-Interest Groups

John Hyland

The participation of postsecondary educational institutions in
community-based programs is a challenge. It involves risk, ambiguity,
and uncertainty. It offers the opportunity to reach people, frequently
adults, who are usually not reached by traditional on-campus programs. It fosters change in the participating institutions. Both the
rewards and the problems are greater than the usual campus-based
programs. It is not an easy or uncomplicated panacea for the problem
of falling enrollments among the traditional college-age population.

The focus of this chapter is on the *organized* aspect of community-
based educational programs — that is, how these programs can deal
with communities as centers of organized ethnic, racial, religious,
social, and cultural groups which are looked at as "special-interest
groups." This approach to community-based education is not to be
confused with programs that have brought people together through a
shotgun recruiting effort. Rather, this approach is based on working
with already organized groups who negotiate a program with the college or who respond to a program offering as an organized constituency.

S. V. Martorana, W. E. Piland (Eds.). *Designing Programs for Community Groups.*
New Directions for Community Colleges, no. 45. San Francisco: Jossey-Bass, March 1984.

The program can take place on campus as well as off, but when community groups connect with higher education institutions in an organized way, the result often is "on-site" education—that is, education in the community.

This chapter advocates such an approach (under certain conditions) and points out elements that foster or prevent its success. Let us begin with an image or scene.

The scene is of a forest, a meadow, and another forest. One forest is inhabited by various tribes—special-interest groups or communities based on ethnicity, class, religion, or culture. On the other side of the meadow, in the other forest, are other tribes—higher education institutions. The meadow is the open area, a kind of "no man's land," undefined, an area to be negotiated.

The tribes of each forest, while not homogeneous, have developed a general consensus about reality. They have constructed and established their own taken-for-granted worlds, routines, traditions, and myths. In each forest the tribes are stratified; they contend with each other for the good things of their world; they cooperate and compete.

These two sets of groups have heard of each other; they have even had some contact in the past. Increasingly now, for a variety of reasons on both sides, they are sending scouts and official representatives out into the meadow to negotiate joint ventures. From the point of view of the higher education institutions, this is an attempt to "connect with the community."

The focus in this chapter is on the encounter in the meadow— that is, on the negotiations, the organizing of working relationships. The major premise is that it is important not to assume too much, not to become "ethnocentric," not to assume that one's own agenda is *the* agenda. In such cooperative ventures, power, money, and status must all be negotiated; there will be some cooperation, some conflict, and the likelihood of compromise and cooperation. It is important for both groups to recognize that these elements will be present in varying degrees, that this does not mean that the negotiations will not be fruitful, but that there will be trade-offs, exchanges, benefits on both sides, as well as disappointments, frustrations, and failures. The encounter in the meadow is risky, exciting, and worthwhile.

LaGuardia Community College (City University of New York) recently celebrated its tenth anniversary. Since it is a familiar "tribe," its experience will serve as a major source of examples—not necessarily exemplary models. From the beginning, LaGuardia has been involved in a series of community-related and sometimes community-based programs. The students in the programs have been members of special-interest groups. Often they came to the college (or the college went out and worked with them) as an organized group, distinct from the general student body who came as a mass of individuals. Frequently, these programs have involved negotiations for modifying the general educational program, for tailoring new forms of higher education to the particular needs of these special-interest groups.

Among the most significant programs with special-interest groups were: (1) the Education Association program for school para-professionals, arranged with the Board of Education and the United Federation of Teachers; (2) the veterans program, involving the Veterans Administration; (3) prisoner programs, with and at the Queens House of Detention; (4) Project Impact, an eighteen-credit program for community leadership, with three community organizations; (5) the program at District Council 37 (the New York City municipal workers union); (6) the program at Solidaridad Humana, a community organization in the lower east side of Manhattan; (7) the program at the National Congress of Neighborhood Women in Brooklyn; (8) the community history project run out of the Social Science Department and reaching into many neighborhoods; (9) the small-business training program for recent immigrants, taught in Spanish and Greek at nearby community centers; and (10) the family daycare training program, which ran courses and workshops all over New York City.

Conceptual Framework

In order to extract meaning from this wealth of experience, community education can benefit from several theoretical perspectives. The work of Randall Collins (1975, 1979) has provided an overall social context for examining the relations of college and community. Collins stresses stratification, organization, and conflict. Groups are in unequal positions in society. They organize in order to struggle for what they consider the good things of life. Education, offering knowledge, skills, and credentials, is a resource in that struggle. Connecting college and community, then, is not only an educational enterprise but also a political, economic, and cultural one.

About thirty years ago, George Simmel (1955) presented several pertinent insights in an essay, "The Web of Group Affiliations." Simmel pointed out that each person is unique in his or her combination of group affiliations and that, because the same person belongs to many groups, he or she stands "at the intersection of social circles." This idea indicates how a person may be approached from several angles — for example, on the basis of class, religion, ethnicity, or culture — and thus how the same population can give rise to several special-interest groups. It also points out that several agendas, sometimes conflicting, may be in operation among and within the groups at any time.

Simmel developed from this notion of intersecting social circles the idea of *cross pressures*. These arise from the fact that, in the complex modern world, the "social circles" of each person are not concentric (and thus in some mutually reinforcing relation) but are often juxtaposed and only partially overlapping.

Paul Lazarsfeld and colleagues (Berelson and others, 1954; Lazarsfeld and others, 1968) developed this concept of cross pressures further by applying it to the study of voting behavior. "By cross pressures we mean the conflicts and inconsistencies among the factors which influence voter decision... In other words, cross pressures upon the voter drive him in opposite directions" (Lazarsfeld and others, 1968, p. 53). Thus, cross pressures are seen as arising from various affiliations (such as religious, occupational, or geographic) and are presented as placing one in a "predicament."

In terms of the college connecting with the community, Simmel and Lazarsfeld indicate how, on the one hand, people may be approached, recruited, or organized from many angles on the basis of their many affiliations or identifications and how, on the other hand, their many affiliations are likely to spark various conflicts.

Philip Selznick's (1949, 1957) work on organizations and Burton Clark's (1956, 1960) elaboration of it in the area of education are extremely helpful in understanding the college-community connection. Selznick stresses the importance of the formation and maintenance of an institution's "organizational character." Organizational character is expressed in the distinctive competencies of the institution, in what it can and cannot do. Selznick and Clark both point out that adaptation to the environment is essential to any organism. However, adaptation must be carried out in such a way as to avoid organizational surrender or co-optation. Clark, in his study of adult education in California, emphasized that this education was becoming so adaptive to the demands of external agencies and populations that it risked having no center, no distinctive competence, and so was very vulnerable. This lesson about adaptation and vulnerability is an important one for both colleges and community groups in the context of negotiations.

Critical Issues

Against the background of these more theoretical points, several key practical issues stand out. A central question is: How are the material and ideal interests of both the college and the community group to be negotiated to bring about a fruitful synthesis? Negotiation is a political process; it is about power. What elements in the final negotiating agenda will be from the agenda of the college and what will be from that of the community group? An additional complicating factor is that there are both institutional agendas and the personal, ideological agendas of the individuals who represent each side. A dean and a community organization director, for example, may agree on a program in principle, but the daily details will be negotiated by a faculty member and a staff person. Personal chemistry becomes important at that point.

A great deal depends on the definition of the college-community relationship in the cooperative venture and of the roles involved. Making a distinction between the formal arrangements and official doctrine on the one hand and the informal processes and operative perceptions on the other hand is useful. Are college and community formally partners and informally adversaries? Are college faculty and the special-interest group's staff colleagues or competitors?

Recognition of the possibility of conflicting agendas and interests leads to the importance of establishing early precise assumptions, expectations, and limitations. What is negotiable? Are admissions policies negotiable? Are courses negotiable? Are modes of instruction negotiable? Is staffing negotiable? Are grading procedures negotiable?

The positive side of these negotiations is the learning that takes place through challenge. Many of our cherished traditions or habits are confronted and questioned by people who have a different world view. We are forced to reexamine curriculum, materials, pedagogy. The change of physical setting through an off-campus program can be a source of new and valuable information. Students, especially adults going to college after many years away from school, may be more comfortable and outspoken in the midst of neighbors or friends on their own physical turf.

Learning from Experience with the National Congress of Neighborhood Women

Several years ago I was teaching an introductory course in social science with the National Congress of Neighborhood Women (NCNW) in Brooklyn. The class was held in a meeting room in the Swinging Sixties Senior Citizens' Center. One day I arrived for class to find the intersection blocked off by the police department. In the middle of the intersection was a table surrounded by a group of women with petitions. Among them were several of my students. They had received notice that morning of a change in eligibility standards for the daycare center that they used. They would be ineligible according to the new criteria, and they were protesting.

When I went to class, a delegation of these students proposed that class be canceled so that all the students could participate in the protest. They justified this proposal with the claim that the NCNW college program was special, that it was meant to provide more than academic abstractions, that it was to be education that had direct application in the lives of the people. On the other hand, there were also students in the class, largely not affected by the daycare crisis, who felt they had waited a long time to go to college and who did not want to miss a class. Supporting the activist students were the staff members of the organization who had a community activist orientation and who were critical of "traditional" academic education. It was a rich example of the negotiated quality of the definition of the learning situation; it shows the interplay of multiple affiliations, agendas, interests, and cross pressures.

In a similar vein, another event indicated the presence of special-interest groups within the special-interest group. NCNW defined itself as feminist, working class, and multiethnic. The main ethnic groups were Italian, Polish, Irish, Puerto Rican, and Black. A colleague had chosen *The Urban Villagers,* a study of an Italian-American neighborhood in Boston written by Herbert Gans (1962), as the main reading for a course. Three days before the course began, a delegation of NCNW staff and students came to a faculty planning meeting to voice their concerns. Some students were opposed to the book because they saw it as part of the "Italianization" of the program: The class was being held in the Italian sector of the neighborhood, in a facility controlled by an Italian block association, by a college named after an Italian, and now a book was being used that continued the focus on Italians. To the faculty it was an extraordinary perception, but it did reveal the power struggles existing within the community.

Working with NCNW was a powerful learning experience. It contained some of the best and the worst aspects of community-based programs. The organization enabled many women to go to college who would not have been able to go under usual circumstances. Many of the women were excellent students who helped make the classes exciting. The program opened up new opportunities for many of the participants, and the college was provided with a bloc of eighty students without having to recruit. There was a cohesiveness to the group, despite its internal divisions, and a built-in support system for the students. NCNW generated a great deal of publicity and visibility for itself and, as a by-product, for the college.

Because of the ideology of the organization and its staff composition, negotiation was sometimes carried to an extreme and trust was sometimes lacking. NCNW saw itself as an agency for social change, combatting the inequalities connected with class, gender, and ethnicity. It had an advocacy style that sometimes made potential allies into adversaries. Its interests as a community organization sometimes conflicted with its role as an educational agency. It very much had its own agenda into which it tried to fit LaGuardia.

Through this program, LaGuardia's faculty members were made more aware of the problems of the adult student, especially of the juggling of college, family, community, and work responsibilities. They experienced the cross pressures of maintaining academic standards (a pressure stemming from their supervisors at the college) and of adapting to an "innovative, special" program (a pressure coming from the community organization).

Comparing the NCNW Program with Other Programs

It is useful to compare the other special-interest group programs with NCNW. They have usually been considered more successful by many administrators and faculty, at least in the sense that they have involved less negotiating and less conflict. With the Education Association program, the college provided sections of traditional courses and some innovative courses at convenient times. With the veterans program, the college provided courses and counseling. With the prison program, Project Impact, and District Council 37, the college provided courses at the site of the special-interest group.

Overall, these programs had agendas that coincided more closely with what the college was used to doing than the NCNW program, and these groups were more accepting of the college's authority in the area of higher education. They were less interested in challenging and changing the college and more focused on getting what the college could offer. However, even in these programs, there were conflicts and accommodations. The union became involved, for example, when its members as students complained of excessive work and strict grading. Students in special-interest group programs often have advocates that students in regular programs do not have.

In the prison program, intervention by a third party, the Correction Department staff, played a reverse role. The college sought optimal conditions for security. For example, it was necessary to arrange a schedule of classes that would take into account prison meal times, security checks, and trips to court. Faculty were required to attend an orientation session given by the Correction Department staff that emphasized security precautions. There was concern that prison guards would be hostile to prisoners who were receiving educational opportunities not available to them. There were questions regarding prerequisites. Since prisoners would not be completing the whole degree program while in that particular detention house, there were requests to waive prerequisites so that the prisoners might be able to take the courses that interested them. Prison staff members were concerned that material that encouraged prisoner discontent or unrest be excluded from course materials. Different priorities led again, at times, to conflict, negotiation, and accommodation. In a sense, the college had learned through the NCNW experience to accept its own limitations and to recognize the degree of flexibility and the capacity for innovation that existed within its staff and in the total social environment.

Two other groups are sometimes involved in the negotiations between community and college. One is the government through its educational agencies. LaGuardia and NCNW, for example, parted company when the New York State Education Department passed regulations limiting the number of courses that could be offered off campus. The education department claimed to be reacting against some institutions that were using diluted off-campus programs to bolster student enrollment. When LaGuardia started to conform to the new regulations, NCNW charged that it was betraying its original commitment and shifted its program to Empire State College, State University of New York. Similarly, federal regulations and appropriations can set limits to the college-community connection.

Funding sources, public and private, also influence the negotiations. The small-business training program for recent immigrants had two agendas. The college's and the community's agenda was focused on skills for people interested or involved in small businesses. The funding source's interest was mainly in the teaching of English as a second language. The program had to be worked out so that both sets of goals could be satisfied.

In the noncredit area, the community history program at LaGuardia stands as a hopeful example. Beginning with an academic course in neighborhood history, the program allowed social science faculty members to establish connections through students and community-involved staff with a widening network of community organizations, especially senior citizens' centers and neighborhood history associations. A planning grant and two implementation grants from the National Endowment for the Humanities has supported the program for four years. Local residents participate by sharing family photographs and documents and by being interviewed for oral histories. Faculty and residents have produced three community history calendars and numerous exhibits in churches, banks, and factories, on subway platforms, at street fairs, and in taverns. Some of this material is now being developed into the Queens County Historical Archives. In this program, the fit between the project's agenda and the community's has been so close that conflicts have been almost nonexistent.

In all of these programs, both credit and noncredit, the social science department has played a major curriculum and staffing role, partly because of the content of its disciplines and partly because of the community orientation of its faculty. Administratively, LaGuardia's Division of Continuing Education has had the major responsibility. In general, this arrangement has worked well enough, although at times program administrators and academic faculty have had to go through the conflict-negotiation-accommodation process themselves.

Influence of the Institution's Orientation

The overall institutional climate is also an important factor in community-based programs. During the first five years of LaGuardia's existence, there was a great emphasis on service to the community in an innovative way. It was in the college's interests to expand its student enrollment on all fronts, to be flexible, to make new arrangements. As a new institution, there was little or no tradition, which sometimes acts as a constraint. In fact, the college was attempting to make innovative community service a central part of its tradition.

In 1975–1976, the national fiscal crisis hit New York City in full force. In this climate, community programs were threatened because of cutbacks, but they were also especially valued if they were funded by other than tax-levy money. Grant support helped compensate for the cutbacks.

In recent years, while the doomsday atmosphere has passed, there has been the cloud of "planned shrinkage" for all New York City services. This has led to greater attention to the limitations of the college's capacity to respond. Community programs are still valued and supported but with more carefulness; the days of the "blue sky" are gone, at least for the time being. Good intentions have been replaced by cost-benefit analyses. This element of the institutional climate—its stage of development in relation to the larger socioeconomic structures and processes—is an important consideration in planning college-community ventures.

The fact that LaGuardia is a cooperative education college has also been helpful to its community orientation. Full-time day students serve three internships with companies or agencies as part of their academic program. This flow between internship and classroom aids in providing an outward thrust to program development and sensitizes staff to educational possibilities in the private sector and in the workplace as a whole.

Obviously, LaGuardia does not have a monopoly on community programs. Three other institutions that have been stimulating in this area are the Highlander Folk School in Tennessee (Adams, 1972), the College for Human Services in New York City (Grant and Riesman, 1978), and Pratt Institute's Center for Community Development in Brooklyn, New York.

A Valuable Approach

The approach of Paulo Freire (1970a, 1970b, 1973, 1978), a Brazilian educator who has also worked in Chile and Guinea-Bissau, provides important suggestions for community-based programs. Freire's philosophy and practice were developed very much in the context of social struggle. Here we describe how the stages of his approach are applied to adult literacy and postliteracy projects.

The educators in his programs work as an interdisciplinary team that ordinarily includes an economist, a sociologist, and a psychologist. Once the area in which they will be working is determined and they have acquired a preliminary acquaintance with it through secondary sources, the first stage begins. Initial contacts are made with individuals of the area, and informal meetings are held to explain the objectives and methods of the program. If a significant number of people agree to the program, then volunteers are sought to be part of the team. The team members begin their own visits to the area, observing various moments in the life of the people — such as work situations, meetings of local associations and clubs, leisure activities, and family situations.

The second stage consists of meetings in which the team members evaluate their experiences, trying to draw out the main themes and contradictions. Codifications (such as sketches or photographs) of these contradictions are developed. These initially aid the team to have a "perception of their previous perception."

Once the codifications have been prepared, the third stage is begun. This involves returning to the area to begin decoding dialogues in "thematic investigation circles." In other words, the people, in groups of ten to twenty, are confronted with their own life situations and begin to analyze the dynamics of their lives. These discussions, which take off from the sketches or photographs, are taped for subsequent analysis by the team.

When the decoding in the "circles" or groups has been completed, the team makes a systematic interdisciplinary study of their findings. Listening to the tapes and studying any notes of reactions from the sessions, the team members compile a list of themes. These are classified according to the social sciences, not in an isolated way but simply to specify the various angles from which to approach each theme. For example, the theme of development could be dealt with from an economic point of view, a sociological one, or a political one. Each specialist develops a breakdown of his or her approach to the themes, putting it into learning units.

The fifth stage is the final preparation of codifications and materials — photographs, slides, film strips, records, tapes, and books.

With all this done, the educators are ready to represent to the people the thematics of their community in systematized and amplified forms. The themes that have come from the people return to them, not as contents to be deposited in them but as problems to be worked on and solved by them.

Conclusion

Connecting with the community by understanding communities as special-interest groups is valuable, exciting, and problematic. Community-related programs are a valid way of providing higher education. They pose different and sometimes additional problems for educators because they often expose dimensions of education that can be hidden by our accustomed ways. They reveal that education is involved in stratification conflict and thus is not neutral. They confront us with negotiations and power struggles on all levels. They challenge our cherished beliefs and customs. They offer us satisfaction and frustration. They show us how good we can be and how much more we need to learn. Whether we volunteer to go out into the meadow or whether we are driven out by circumstances beyond our control, we can bring back great riches for our tribe.

References

Adams, F. "Highlander Folk School: Getting Information, Going Back and Teaching It." *Harvard Educational Review,* 1972, *42* (4), 497–520.

Berelson, B. R., Lazarsfeld, P. F., and McPhee, W. N. *Voting.* Chicago: University of Chicago Press, 1954.

Clark, B. R. *Adult Education in Transition.* Berkeley: University of California Press, 1956.

Clark, B. R. *The Open-Door College.* New York: McGraw-Hill, 1960.

Collins, R. *Conflict Sociology.* New York: Academic Press, 1975.

Collins, R. *The Credential Society.* New York: Academic Press, 1979.

Freire, P. *Cultural Action for Freedom.* Monograph Series No. 1. Cambridge, Mass.: Harvard Educational Review and Center for the Study of Development and Social Change, 1970a.

Freire, P. *Pedagogy of the Oppressed.* (M. B. Ramos, trans.) New York: Seabury Press, 1970b.

Freire, P. *Education for Critical Consciousness.* (M. B. Ramos, trans.) New York: Seabury Press, 1973.

Freire, P. *Pedagogy in Process.* (C. Hunter, trans.) New York: Seabury Press, 1978.

Gans, H. J. *The Urban Villagers.* New York: Macmillan, 1962.

Grant, G., and Riesman, D. "The College for Human Services." *The Perpetual Dream; Reform and Experiment in the American College.* Chicago: University of Chicago Press, 1978.

Lazarsfeld, P. F., Berelson, B. R., and Gaudet, H. *The People's Choice.* New York: Columbia University Press, 1968. (Originally published 1944).

Selznick, P. *TVA and the Grass Roots.* Berkeley: University of California Press, 1980. (Originally published 1949).

Selznick, P. *Leadership in Administration.* New York: Harper & Row, 1957.

Simmel, G. "The Web of Group Affiliations." In G. Simmel, *Conflict and the Web of Group Affiliations.* (K. H. Wolff and R. Bendix, trans.) New York: Free Press, 1955.

John Hyland is professor and chairperson of the social service department at LaGuardia Community College, City University of New York.

The concern that exists in all localities about the health of their economic base can become a rallying point for areawide cooperation among community groups.

Joining Others for Community Economic Development

Joseph A. Borgen
William B. Shade

Although much has been written about the practice of community economic development and about the roles, actual or potential, of community organizations and leaders in that development, these subjects continue to hold special significance for community college program builders. Since most community economic development programs are organized through a dominant chamber of commerce or a separate economic development organization, they present an excellent opportunity for cooperation among these community groups and the area's community college. To demonstrate how such a cooperative venture might work, this chapter looks first at the basic principles of economic development and then presents a case study.

Economic development is often used interchangeably with the term *industrial development*. Economic development is defined differently by different persons. A business person may use this term to mean increasing business investment; a citizen may think of creating jobs in a community. To others, it means recruiting new industry, retaining existing enterprise, or growing new companies via entrepreneurial development. In this chapter, economic development is viewed as community

S. V. Martorana, W. E. Piland (Eds.). *Designing Programs for Community Groups.*
New Directions for Community Colleges, no. 45. San Francisco: Jossey-Bass, March 1984.

leadership activities designed to retain, recruit, and create (through entrepreneurship) primary economic jobs for the area.

Primary economic jobs are those for which money, contracts, and orders come from outside an area and from which products or services leave the area. Primary jobs create wealth and can be referred to as "value adding." Primary jobs exist, for example, in businesses engaged in intrastate or interstate commerce for purposes of manufacturing, processing, or assembling products, in commercial research and development, and in providing services in interstate commerce. Manufacturing, farming, mining, and forestry are the most common categories of primary economic activity.

Secondary economic jobs exist in an area due to the money circulating from primary employment. Examples include retail employment, banking, auto sales, education, construction, health services, and professional services. Again, significant community economic development and growth result from increasing primary, value-adding employment.

What could be the goals of an economic development project? One of the goals might be simply to maintain or recover the manufacturing jobs that have been lost in an area. A second goal might go beyond that of recovering and maintaining to expanding business and the number of jobs in the community. The second goal can be more controversial than the first. It is difficult to envision anyone being against the first goal (that is, recovering and maintaining the economic level of the community with regard to manufacturing). It is understandable that some may have concerns about goals that would substantially increase the size of an area and build the requirements for an expanded infrastructure in the community.

Why Engage in Economic Development:
Will Our Economy Simply Recycle?

Most economists and citizens know that our economy works in cycles: We have a few years of increased activity and employment, followed by a brief recession to cool off; then we regroup and go on to a higher level of economic activity. Bankers, people in small businesses, realtors, and almost everyone else now know that we have been on the down side of a cycle for a number of years. The question is: Will we recycle back and exceed past economic levels in agriculture, business, manufacturing, construction, and so on? There are those now who say that the cycle will not be repeated this time, at least in regions of the Midwest and in segments of our economy such as manufacturing, transportation, and steel.

A bit of recent economic history gives another perspective. At the end of World War II, the United States was the major undamaged free country in the world. There was no destruction of our cities or our factories. We had a very small loss of manpower, about three hundred thousand American lives as compared to about four million in Germany and twenty million in Russia. The four great powers, Germany, Japan, Russia, and England, were devastated; they had no economy, and their labor force was exhausted. As a result, the United States entered the greatest economic boom that the world has ever known following World War II, and experienced a tremendous expansion of its markets because of the lack of international competition. The world was hungering for its products; there were demands that could not be met.

During that period, there were substantial increases in the cost of labor. The cost of products did not produce inflation during the 1950s and 1960s because there were productivity increases in the magnitude of 3.5 percent to 5.0 percent a year. During this same period, the United States was putting a substantial amount of capital into the rebuilding of both Europe and Japan.

Our recent history shows that we are now experiencing international competition from Japan, Germany, and the rest of Europe. Our country has lost significant parts of industries like television, apparel, shoes, optics, motorcycles, and watches, and the Germans, Japanese, and Swedish have taken over 30 percent of our domestic automobile market.

Instead of having from a 3.0 percent ot a 5.0 percent increase in industrial productivity as in the 1950s and 1960s, the United States has lost productivity increases in the industries of our country. From 1968 to 1978, the U.S. Department of Labor indicated a net gain of 23.6 percent in industrial productivity for our economy. In Japan, the productivity increase for the same ten-year period was 89.1 percent; in Germany, it was 63.8 percent; in Holland, 93.7 percent; and in Italy, 60.1 percent. The United States has fallen to tenth among all nations in per-capita gross national product — down five slots in one year. We are, in part, competing now in the international markets with economies that built most of their plants substantially after World War II.

In looking at the changing structure of our national economy and at international competition, we can see that the future is not going to be like the past. In short, we cannot take for granted that we will automatically come back into a growth or expansion period on the up side of the cycle. The times are different. Energy is very expensive and growing in cost. Deregulation of natural gas and severance tax on coal will add to the competitive disadvantage of parts of the country, and raw materials are finite.

Thus, a concern about the economic future of the country in which we live, of our communities, businesses, and families, has spurred an intense interest in economic development. In fact, there appears to be a significant change in the political mood of both major parties — a desire to focus on the creation of wealth (that is, on economic development) and to turn away from the preoccupation with the distribution of wealth that was characteristic of the last three decades.

Why Should an Area Strengthen Economic Development Efforts?

There are many motivations for a community to participate in economic development. Some stronger ones are presented briefly here.

Regain Lost Manufacturing Employment and Other Primary Jobs. The United States Chamber of Commerce estimates that 100 manufacturing jobs mean about one million dollars in annual bank deposits, $250,000 in new-car sales, $300,000 annual grocery sales, and forty to sixty additional jobs in the community. For every 100 manufacturing jobs that we lose or gain in a community, we can subtract or add their economic effects. In short, economic development is good for banks, retail establishments, newspapers, schools, doctors, lawyers, job seekers (obviously), and anyone who is involved in one way or another with the local economy.

Spread the Tax Base for Existing Industries, Farmers, Businesses, and Property Owners. One can argue that the continued migration of industrial enterprises out of a community and the lack of primary employment are "push factors" on taxes for farmers and existing industries; that is, the expansion of primary employment can help spread the tax base and load while a shrinking tax base can increase pressure on the remaining payers.

Broaden the Economic Diversity of the Area. More economic diversity helps protect businesses from the impact of one economic sector's down side of the curve.

Provide Employment Opportunities. Finding or creating jobs for young people and the unemployed is, of course, beneficial to the whole community.

Avoid Depending on the Chance That Our Economy Will Improve. Taking action to improve the economy is a positive, aggressive step that local people can make. The federal government or state government will not do it for a community. Communities themselves must resolve to develop their own economies.

What Is the Nature of Economic
Decision Making?

If the purpose of economic development is to increase primary employment, then economic development decisions are business decisions made by business men and women. They are not decisions made by legislators, governors, cities, or schools, although the activities of these people and organizations can be of influence. Decision making is accomplished in an environment that acknowledges both domestic and international business competition. Decisions are based on a variety of factors that are given differing values by individual companies. But no matter what is on the list of specific decision-making factors, the final consideration is profit and relative productivity. In other words, where does it make the most sense to do business profitably?

The task of an economic development program is to market, sell, and advocate the area as an attractive place to do business, to locate a new plant or enterprise, or to expand an existing enterprise. The task is to communicate primarily with corporate executives — the top management leaders both of firms that reside in an area and of new companies that fit the economic goals of the area. These corporate executives are interested in finance, investment, training, transportation, industrial sites, facilities, governmental services, utilities, energy, labor supply, taxes, and the quality of life. They are interested in affinity to markets, supplies, and raw materials.

Economic development discussions, then, are between key leaders in an area and corporate executives — that is, the top management leaders responsible for strategic business decisions.

Marketing a community is similar to selling anything in that the more prospects one can talk with, the better the chances are for a "sale." Investing many dollars in domestic if not international marketing of an area is common in communities that are aggressive in economic development. A clear goal and plan are essential to secure the types of enterprises that best fit a particular geographical area.

The communities that are most effective in advocating themselves are those that are best able to provide competitive incentives and good information on all fronts. In short, the advantage goes to the prepared. Practical experience persuades us that a team of advocates working with corporate clients to address the interests of the corporations can be very effective. Effective teams from an area should include top decision makers from local government, financial institutions, businesses, training and educational institutions, and state government. Discussions are confidential, often at the insistence of potential corporate clients, since they involve proprietary interests and strategic plans.

Community and technical college leaders have a valuable and unique role to perform as an economic development team advocate. Corporate prospects are intently concerned about the numbers and skills of the work force in an area. Training tailored to meet the specific needs of a company is always a key incentive in selling an area as a good place to locate a company. A track record of satisfying the training needs of existing companies is always impressive. Specific assistance in applying the benefits of federal and state training resources, such as the Job Partnership Training Act (JPTA), to a specific company's plans can be a competitive incentive. The willingness to be flexible with regard to training sites, formats, and strategies, together with creative, aggressive ideas for helping a company be productive, profitable, and competitive, are assets in helping to sell an area.

Again, economic development is practiced in a competitive environment. Most often, a business will consider, in the final analysis, four to six areas for expansion. They will compare community offers related to start-up training, sites, facilities, financing, affinity to markets, business climate, transportation, labor supply, quality of life, and other factors. Community and technical college leaders can make effective area advocates. In the final analysis, the advantage in economic development goes to those areas that are best prepared to be effective advocates on all fronts, including that of training.

The following is a case study of an economic development effort in a midwestern city. This study illustrates a team approach to economic development with a community-based, postsecondary institution playing a prominent role in the effort. A variety of special-interest groups—including business, labor, the unemployed, and the local chamber of commerce—were served by this economic development approach. The case study does not present an in-depth treatment of the complexities of regional economic development processes. Instead, it stresses the functional elements of a human resource and economic development effort in Terre Haute, Indiana, that has led to the formulation of a communitywide work-force development project.

Case Study: Economic Development in Terre Haute, Indiana

The first part of this case study presents a summary of Terre Haute's history, providing a conceptual base for understanding the community. Then we analyze the project's genesis, its organizational structure, the needs assessment, and the survey methodology. The case study is concluded by touching briefly on some possible spinoff projects of the Terre Haute model and its implications for educators, employers, students, community residents, and cooperative education job developers.

The overall characteristics of the Terre Haute community and neighboring Vigo County had to be recognized and dealt with if the objectives of an economic development project were to be attained. Some of the special considerations were factually demographic, some involved image, some were attitudinal, and some displayed a cause-and-effect nature. The paragraphs that follow are paraphrased from Rust's (1975) compilative work on American urban centers.

Historical Background of Terre Haute. The city was an early frontier outpost. Steamer traffic on the Wabash River began in 1818 and prospered through most of the nineteenth century. The city was a river port for the grain, pork, and whiskey of the region. Historical population figures for the Standard Metropolitan Statistical Area (SMSA) show steady growth into the 1920s; much of this growth was in the rural and small-town population outside Terre Haute proper. Some iron and steel were made using local coal and ore, and paper was made from local straw. Coal mining boomed in the region before 1900, followed closely by a glass-blowing industry (which originated the classic Coca Cola bottle in 1911), brick and ceramic pipe works, and the maintenance shops of the Pennsylvania Railroad. The four-county region grew rapidly on the coal boom to a 1920 population of 189,000.

In a few years after World War I, the railroad maintenance shops were shut down; the breweries and distilleries were closed because of the Eighteenth Amendment; papermaking was abandoned; and local iron, steel, and ceramic industries entered a long decline. Coal mining collapsed in the late 1920s. The region's population has remained near 175,000 ever since, despite sporadic attempts to resuscitate the local economy.

The Depression was extremely hard on the Terre Haute area: Its employment was severely reduced, but its population remained steady. The impact was greatest in heavy industry with its preponderance of male employees. There may have been an influx of female-employing, low-wage employers such as canneries at this time. In any case, the percentage of women in the area's total employment rose from well below average in 1930 to near average in 1940 and has stayed there since.

Terre Haute's distilling and heavy manufacturing base was largely gone by 1940. The area had declined in population since before 1920 but had remained a significant trade and service center with considerable food-processing employment and a large coal-mining sector in the outlying parts of the SMSA. Despite the closing of the Pennsylvania Railroad's western maintenance shops at Terre Haute, the percentage of railroad employment was still significantly higher than the national average.

Although the decade of the 1940s was relatively prosperous for the Terre Haute area, the 1950s were disastrous; the agriculture, mining, railroad transportation, and food-processing industries each shed several thousand jobs, while even wholesale trade, retail trade, communication, and government showed losses. Only the electrical machinery sector expanded significantly, but it was far from enough to prevent a decline in total employment.

The 1960s were not as bad as the previous decade, but they showed no real departure from the established pattern. Mining, agriculture, food products, and the railroad continued to decline; trade and most services failed to keep pace with the expansive trends in the 1960s (the exception being a major expansion of Indiana State University); and manufacturing grew, notably paper, chemicals, and electrical machinery. The loss of population that was triggered by the distress of the 1950s, combined with some growth of employment, made for improved income per capita; nevertheless unemployment and underemployment generated by the declining sectors contributed to a poverty level of 9.6 percent in 1969.

Vigo County along with Clay, Sullivan, and Vermillion Counties comprise the Terre Haute SMSA, which is located along the Illinois border in West Central Indiana. A digest of 1970 population and housing conditions shows an old, stable population, often poor but strongly inclined toward home ownership and with exceptionally low-valued stock of owner-occupied housing.

The population of Vigo County peaked in the early 1970s. A slow decrease was forecast at least through the year 2000. Most significantly, Vigo County population, as a percent of the total state population, peaked at 3.42 percent in the 1920s; that percentage has decreased slowly and will continue to decrease to about 1.8 percent by 2000. The age-group demographics for the 1980–1990 decade indicate further aggravation of the situation. At the time that the economic development project was initiated, Terre Haute was well on its way to becoming a "former city." Drastic communitywide action was required to alter these trends.

Image. Like many other cities throughout the world, Terre Haute has had problems in overcoming some negative popular perceptions of its character. Prohibition, open ordinances, corrupt politicians, and police created some unpleasant features in the environment in the early decades of this century. Unfortunately, the implications of those features tended to linger and foster negative impressions. Such denigration fed on itself and thwarted the much-needed building of a positive image.

At the time of the economic development project, the community, as a whole, seemed to have a relatively low self-image. It seemed willing to accept "half a loaf" when more was really available at the local, state, and federal levels. The conditions of city streets and railroad crossings reflected acceptance of low expectations. A "bootstrap" effort to eliminate the defeatist syndrome was essential if a further downhill slide was to be averted.

Attitudes. In general, attitudes in the community were basically individualistic: "I'm O.K. Why worry?" Political strengths were high with much more emphasis on political party success than on overall community success. By the same token, the labor constituency apparently placed more emphasis on the individual than on the total community. The "it can't happen to me" feeling was widely evident, reinforced by a "we made it through before, so we'll do it again" attitude. But in the face of the community's economic trends, continued complacency would have been a tragedy. An extensive public education effort was seen as essential to alert the community to the real danger ahead.

It is important to differentiate between cause and effect. Extensive effort has gone into a variety of local projects aimed at treating the cause of the community's current status or the effects of those causes. Unfortunately, the majority of that effort has been placed on treating the symptoms rather than the problem.

The primary causes for deterioration in the Terre Haute and Vigo County area were failure to develop competitive advantages, artificial barriers to free competition, arbitrary or politically motivated actions, and lack of real leadership in the past. It can be argued that the demographics are in part cause and in part effect. But the demographics are real; changing those trends, in a very broad sense, will require making the community more attractive than the areas to which Terre Haute citizens are migrating. The inability to develop barge navigation on the Wabash River downstream from Terre Haute and the lack of interest in developing the freight-forwarding potential (rail and air) that existed — because of the geographic relationships between Terre Haute and the major markets of the mid-west — have caused the loss of competitive advantages in both the industrial and business areas. These and other causes had to be addressed forcefully by the economic development project. A reordering of priorities was imperative.

Project Recommended by Industry. The idea for the Community-wide Work Force Development Project was conceived by the Chamber of Commerce's Existing Industry Council (CCEIC), chaired by the president of the Terre Haute Area Chamber of Commerce. The council, which is comprised of representatives from the major manufacturing firms in Terre Haute and the surrounding Vigo County, meets regularly to address issues and problems affecting business and industry in the Greater Terre Haute Area. One such issue is existing industry's concern over the future lack of availability of skilled, professional, and semiskilled labor caused by expected industrial expansion and a general migration of the area's young people for career opportunities elsewhere.

In 1979, a population analysis of the Greater Terre Haute Area revealed a continuing decrease in the number of high school graduates and a decreasing labor pool due to an unusually large number of older employees who would be retiring from the current labor pool over the next few years. Unless corrected, the council realized that these trends would most certainly have a detrimental effect not only on Terre Haute's ability to attract new industry into the area but also on its ability to retain existing industry.

In addition, forecasts for the decade of the 1980s, based on demographic data, indicate some very real problems for Vigo County and Terre Haute. While the United States as a whole can expect a 10 percent increase in total population, Indiana can expect only 4 percent. At the same time, Vigo County's population will shrink slightly. County population in the fifteen- to twenty-four-year-old age group will drop about 15.4 percent while the twenty-five- to forty-four-year-old age group will increase by 26.2 percent. Significantly, census data comparing 1968 and 1978 figures show that employment grew by 15 percent over that ten-year period with the only significant decrease being in the Transportation and Public Utility area. According to census data, although the Terre Haute SMSA is considered to be depressed, the area's broad diversity of manufacturing operations provides a stability not present in single-industry communities. As a consequence, the unemployment rates for this area are below average for the state. In sum, the economic climate would be highly vulnerable to a continued decrease in persons available for the area work force.

The Communitywide Work Force Development Project was created from existing industry's plan to stabilize the labor force and to accommodate economic growth. The project consists of an action plan involving industry, education, and government. Its goal is to create a mechanism within the Greater Terre Haute Area and Vigo County that is capable of meeting the quantitative and qualitative work-force needs of the employing community. The project represents a commitment on the part of industry in the Greater Terre Haute Area to participate actively in a skills development program.

Organizational Structure of the Project. The Existing Industry Council suggested that Indiana State University's (ISU) Cooperative Professional Practice program could serve as an effective tool in solving some of the problem, particularly if it could be coordinated with experiential learning programs offered by other educational institutions in the community. The council felt that ISU's Professional Practice program would provide a structured framework around which to cluster other forms of experiential learning—such as distributive and vocational education at the high school level, cooperative education, career education, summer employment programs, and internships. As that framework develops, special consideration projects, such as employment of the handicapped, programs for adult women wishing to enter or reenter the work force, minority employment programs, and apprentice training programs, could be integrated into the cluster.

Thus, the Communitywide Work Force Development Project was approved in September 1980 by the Chamber of Commerce's Board of Directors, is admininistered by Indiana State University's Cooperative Professional Practice program, and is operating as part of the chamber's economic development effort to meet the skilled labor needs of the Greater Terre Haute Area.

Funding. The Existing Industry Council provided initial seed money for the Work Force Development Project by soliciting financial contributions from major area employers. The seed money covered the costs of the initial project design and its implementation, but in the long run, the project will have to exist on community resources. The industry contributions have, in fact, been kept to a minimum so that funding can be shifted to a communitywide support base as soon as is practical. The council estimates that it will take about three years of implementation effort to develop a system that will produce more value for the community than it costs to operate.

Staffing. The labor-intensive portions of this project occur during the initial survey of the existing work force and subsequently at intervals when change information is solicited. Project staffing includes one full-time professional, a half-time graduate assistant, a half-time project director, and a contact staff of students from high schools, community colleges, and Indiana State University. The project director provides program guidance with the assistance of an advisory council from the employing community and of a recently appointed coordinating committee from the education and training community.

It is worth noting, also, that involving area high schools and their students in the project is aimed at increasing student awareness of the need for early career planning and at maximizing the effectiveness of high school career counseling and career exploration.

Budget. For such staffing, an initial budget of approximately $4,500 per month was required. Implementation was projected to require three years, at which time the project was to have proven itself and thereby become a community-supported effort. Precise budget estimates for future years would be based on development and implementation experience of the first year. For forward planning purposes, however, the annual budget was projected on a plus 13 percent basis, a figure that was in line with the current factoring governing the economy.

Advisory Council. A ten-person advisory council consisting of top officials from business and industry, city and county government, and education was formed to set goals and objectives, identify work assignments, and monitor the progress of the program. Subsumed under the advisory council were four planned committees with the following project responsibilities:

1. Training Resources Committee — to identify all educational programs, agencies, and organizations providing skill training or related services. An end result of this committee's work was the development of a comprehensive Directory of Training Resources for communitywide usage.

2. Training Evaluation Committee — to evaluate training curricula at the community college and university level. This committee would visit four-year colleges, technical institutes, vocational schools, high schools, and community colleges located within the maximum labor-draw area of Terre Haute. They would examine courses offered, program content, and enrollments. An end result of this committee's work was a series of recommendations on ways to improve the quantity of educational programs to meet local industry's and graduates' needs.

3. Training Equipment Coordination Committee — to develop a total inventory of surplus equipment and manufacturing products available through area companies that could be used for training purposes by high schools, technical institutes, and two-year and four-year colleges.

4. Promotion and Publicity Committee — to promote job opportunities in local business and industry. The committee developed brochures to describe area business operations and to identify specific job opportunities available in major area companies. This committee would have responsibility for information dissemination to educators, students, parents, and others interested in areawide career and job opportunities.

Needs Assessment. Developing an instrument for surveying current and projected skilled labor requirements in the Greater Terre Haute Area was one of the initial activities of the Communitywide Work Force Development Project. Both educators and industry representatives recognized the need to identify the specific skill requirements of employers in the Terre Haute area — information necessary to design and implement effective campus-based and employer-based training curricula. It was agreed that all employing organizations, industrial and nonindustrial, having one or more employees would be surveyed.

Survey Method. Initially, 108 employers in the Greater Terre Haute Area were mailed a survey and asked to identify current and anticipated job openings, at calendar intervals, in skilled, professional, semiskilled, technical, and unskilled areas over the next five years and in over forty-one job categories. A list of occupational titles and definitions for skilled production and technical support jobs was provided. These skilled occupations were those that generally require at least a high school diploma in addition to specific vocational or technical training at the high school or community college level. The survey was not designed to measure the total job needs of area employers but rather to identify those critical skilled jobs that require both academic and special vocational training.

Plant visits were made to most of the companies participating in the survey, since every company in the area has an impact on skilled labor supply and demand. Production operations were observed to ensure that jobs were properly classified, and interviews were held with management staff to determine realistic projected employment needs.

The survey instrument was also designed to provide wage data. This information is extremely valuable in helping to attract students into training programs and in providing realistic salary expectations when they enter the job market.

After the initial survey, the project calls for an annual assessment to determine the degree of change. It was agreed that such a resurvey would be done on a yearly basis to coincide with each organization's fiscal or planning cycle.

Future Directions. It is obvious that employers are very concerned about education and training. The United States no longer leads the world in advanced technology or productivity. If productivity is to become an American value again, the educational system must do its part.

As human resource and regional economic development professionals in the Greater Terre Haute Area look to the future, cooperative education is very much in their plans. Some possible spinoff projects tied to the Work Force Development Project include:

- Establishing and expanding cooperative educational programs to involve high school and college students in practical work experiences
- Developing a program that offers summer and part-time employment in industry for vocational teachers, counselors, and college professors
- Organizing visits to industry sites for students, parents, and educators
- Broadening and increasing the effectiveness of career-day programs and information dissemination
- Developing a roster of industry personnel to serve as on-campus instructors, particularly in the technical fields
- Serving as liaison with state, county, and national agencies to identify regional needs and funding priorities for related training.

Conclusion

The recurring theme throughout this case study and its major implication for educators, employers, urban planners, and cooperative education job developers lie in the recognition of the increasing interdependency among all sectors of a community and the urgent need for effective communication. Too often the public, private, and educational sectors concerned with a given issue express their views from a narrow or isolated perspective, with cacophony rather than constructive communication the result.

With this project, the Greater Terre Haute Area Chamber of Commerce and the Existing Industry Council have achieved a major breakthrough that should facilitate future attempts to bring different sectors of a community together in a discussion of basic human resource and economic development issues. By encouraging participation and frank expression, the project leaders offer the community participants an opportunity to forge a fruitful coalition for the future.

The economic development and work-force problems in Greater Terre Haute, Indiana, are not peculiar to that metropolitan area. To a lesser or greater extent, they exist throughout the country's urban centers. What appears to be peculiar to the Terre Haute area, however, is the collaborative process used to understand the community by examining its economic development. Success in this project was dependent on organizational and institutional willingness to collaborate and to work together—to do away with jurisdictional disputes and to work for the common good.

The experience, structure, and procedures of this project, therefore, not only are a potential solution to Terre Haute's work-force problems but also can serve as a model for other communities around the country. Modified to fit the economic and demographic characteristics of a particular community, this model can be applied to the economic benefit of a large variety of communities.

Reference

Rust, E. *No Growth: Impacts on Metropolitan Areas.* Lexington, Mass.: Lexington Books, 1975.

Joseph A. Borgen, president of Des Moines Area Community College in Iowa, is vice-chairman of the Greater Des Moines Bureau of Economic Development.

William B. Shade, director of Managerial Recruiting and Cooperative Education Programs, General Motors Corporation, formerly was associate dean for external affairs at General Motors Institute in Michigan.

*The nexus between federal and state interests, on the one
hand, and local communities as centers of action, on the other,
will become increasingly important and more complex over the
next several years. Various techniques can help facilitate the
connections among government and community groups.*

Understanding Communities as Centers of Action for State and Federal Interests

Edward D. Goldberg

Several principles provide a background for understanding communities as centers that promote state and federal interests. These principles essentially assert that implementation is best carried out at the
level closest to the recipient of service. In political science, this principle takes the form of home rule, which asserts that as many functions
as possible ought to be carried out by municipalities and counties as opposed to states or the federal government. There is also a parallel principle from political science that is generally labeled "accountability."
This principle asserts that institutions and agencies ought to be given
the latitude to implement programs without many constraints as long
as there are stringent requirements for reporting on the effectiveness
and efficiency of actions taken. Both these principles support the general
proposition that federal and state interests should be implemented at a
local or regional level and done so with little constraint, other than the
requirement that there be accountability for actions taken.

These two principles from political science can be supplemented
with one from economics and one from business management. Adam

S. V. Martorana, W. E. Piland (Eds.). *Designing Programs for Community Groups.*
New Directions for Community Colleges, no. 45. San Francisco: Jossey-Bass, March 1984.

Smith, in *The Wealth of Nations* (1937), wrote of the greatest good for the greatest number flowing from a decentralized system of economic activity. To a large degree, much of what he wrote about economic activity and what leads to success has meaning for activity in the public sector. If you substitute a bureaucrat in Trenton or Harrisburg or Albany or Washington for Smith's bureaucrat in London, his point still has tremendous validity: Needs can best be responded to by people close to the scene.

A parallel principle from the business world is found in the management philosophy of "decentralization." Although one can cite examples of successful, large-scale, highly centralized corporate efforts in the United States, the best models of business success seem to be those that provide some central direction while allowing decentralized units latitude to pursue specific objectives and implement specific actions.

The principles support the general theme that communities have an important role to play in responding to federal and state interests. In effect, the principles argue that federal and state policy makers would do well to avoid the errors of excessive centralization and instead to create a climate by which their interests are well articulated and mechanisms are established for local implementation.

Overview of Federal and State Interests

Federal and state interests generally occur when there is a need to assure the individual citizen access to relatively uniform services regardless of where that citizen lives, particularly when there are major economies of scale either in planning or operation in an area or when there is a belief that localities and local agencies, left to their own discretion, would not or could not provide services. This reasoning explains federal and state interests regarding the compilation of statistics, the federal court system, the federal social security system, and the federal defense system, to cite a few of hundreds of possible illustrations.

The *Catalogue of Federal Domestic Assistance* (1983, p. 5) illustrates the federal involvement with local concerns. It "is a governmentwide compendium of federal programs, projects, services, and activities that provides assistance or benefits to the American public." It describes 963 financial and nonfinancial assistance programs that provide a wide range of benefits and services. These have been grouped into twenty basic functional categories by primary purpose. The twenty categories are: (1) agriculture; (2) business and commerce; (3) community development; (4) consumer protection; (5) cultural affairs; (6) disaster prevention and relief; (7) education; (8) employment, labor, and training; (9) energy; (10) environmental protection; (11) food and nutrition; (12) health; (13) housing; (14) income security and social services; (15) information and statistics; (16) law, justice, and legal services; (17) natural resources; (18) regional development; (19) science and technology; and (20) transportation.

Similarly, one can find the state involved in fostering human resource training, environmental protection, transportation, economic development, and a wide range of other services. In all these programs, one frequently finds a pragmatic yet patchwork and almost schizophrenic division of responsibility among the various levels of government and other local agencies for functions such as planning, coordination, and operation. Which level is to do what and under what constraints differs by program and subprogram, often without consistency.

What seems clear is that, over the next few years, even with a pruned-back federal budget and financially constrained state budgets, federal and state interests will not diminish. Even the massive federal cutbacks in such programs as Comprehensive Employment Training Act (CETA) two years ago still left federal governmental interests as a major force in human resource development at the local level, and this force continues under the new Job Training Partnership Act. The challenge for communities and local agencies is, therefore, how to respond to these federal and state interests while, at the same time, shaping those interests. How communities and local agencies, including educational institutions, participate in shaping federal and state interests will be important for community college decision makers.

Responding to Federal and State Interests

There are four major steps a college can take to position itself as a center of action for promoting state and federal interests.

Time Management. After establishing the general principle that it is desirable for an institution to implement federal and state interests, the college faces the first step, which is to overcome what is called "Gresham's Law of Planning" (March and Simon, 1958). This law, which parallels the economic principle called "Gresham's Law of Money" (Freedman, 1982), states that attention to immediate, pressing, operational detail prevents consideration of important long-term planning issues. No doubt, the program development decision maker is bombarded daily with much in the way of detail that needs to be responded to because of its immediate, operational nature. But institutions must establish a rather comprehensive process to promote federal and state interests, and without the decision maker and staff being able to set aside significant blocks of time to begin to plan, the planning effort will be less than adequate.

Overcoming Gresham's Law of Planning is not easy but it can be done. There are three ways in which time can be made available for the decision maker through time management: changing the definition of the decision maker's role, changing the nature of the organizational relationships, and changing the personal style of the decision maker. Again, the organizational principle set forth in Gresham's Law is that, without explicit effort, the decision maker will be trapped into dealing only with immediate operating detail.

The first way to reduce rapidly the amount of time a decision maker must work on such detail is to define his or her role in such a way as to narrow its scope. Obviously, changes in the definition of the role will translate into changes in the amount of time required. The management literature (Longenecker, 1973) supports the definition of the decision maker's role as being one that is externally oriented, based on a view of an institution as an "open system"—that is, a system that attempts to survive by relating to the larger environment. Survival, then, becomes a function of the types of exchanges the institution has with its environment as opposed to how it structures itself internally and how its internal processes work. Thus, tasks dealing with interactions, potential employers in job markets, the body of knowledge, and all elements of the local community are the tasks to be given priority by the decision maker. This is not to deny that there is important work to be done in connection with internal matters; this approach just suggests the priority of environmental relationships.

In addition to the "open systems" concept, certain other exhortations in the management literature can be used to narrow the decision maker's role. For instance, decision makers find themselves being reminded of the differences between effectiveness and efficiency (Drucker, 1963) and of the Pareto Principle (Juran, 1965).

In drawing the distinction between effectiveness and efficiency, the decision maker should assign first priority to seeing that the "right" tasks are done as opposed to seeing that tasks are done well. The expression that it does an institution no good to do the wrong thing with 100 percent accuracy reflects the need for the decision maker to be sure he or she is concentrating time on seeing that the "right" tasks are performed. Even an inefficient job on these tasks will be more productive than 100 percent accuracy on the wrong ones. Role definition must be such that emphasis is placed on coming up with satisfactory decisions regarding crucial problems.

The Pareto Principle suggests that a listing of tasks together with their outcomes will show that the completion of a small number will generate the bulk of the value to be gained and that completion of the large number of remaining tasks will generate very little value. This general rule of thumb concerning numbers is to be noted everywhere. Some examples include: a small number of employees cause most disciplinary problems, a small number of inventory items account for most of the value of the total inventory, and a small number of researchers account for the majority of innovations.

For the decision maker, Pareto's Principle suggests that attention to the appropriate small number of items will generate the greatest return to the institution. The problem is to choose the "right" items to work on and to be sure that attention is not given to any item without considering the return on the time invested.

Another major way in which to reduce time demands on the decision maker is to change the nature of organizational relationships. This can be accomplished by reviewing the number of administrators reporting to the decision maker with an eye toward reducing that number and by reviewing the work assignments of subordinates with an eye toward increasing the scope of their work. In simplistic form, the fewer individuals who report and the greater the scope of their work and that of their subordinates, the more time the decision maker will have for high-priority items.

The decision maker's span of control can be reduced easily by fiat. The decision maker finds fewer individuals reporting to him or her since the nature of the hierarchy has been changed. Increased delegation, on the other hand, is harder to implement. It requires subordinates capable of assuming additional responsibilities — capable both in the sense of having the required expertise and in the sense of having the time.

Increased delegation may even require the prior development of various subordinates in order to provide them with increased capabilities, and many institutions are not noted for such developmental activities. Yet development of human resources has to be accomplished so that various functions now performed by the decision maker or directly supervised by him or her can be performed or supervised by others.

Subordinates, to handle the delegated functions, will have to, like the executive, review their role, check their span of control, and delegate more. It is in the institution's best interests that responsibility for certain functions and decisions be moved downward.

There are various techniques for reducing the time demand by changing one's personal style. Most of these techniques are of a rather mundane nature, but they can have major impact.

To avoid wasting time, the decision maker must take steps that save seconds and minutes — units of time that add up to those precious, hopefully uninterrupted, three- to four-hour blocks of time that can be devoted to crucial, long-term matters. Some suggestions are:

- Handle each project item, or memo as few times as possible. Try to complete work on it at one time to avoid having to familiarize yourself with its nature over and over again.
- Prepare an agenda for every meeting to make meetings relatively short.
- Keep a briefcase filled with work handy at all times, so that work can be done during short periods of time that otherwise would be wasted.
- Review all socializing on the job from a cost-benefit perspective.

Further, the trick is to avoid interruptions. If the decision maker can identify characteristics of those incoming messages that are crisis oriented (whether they arrive by phone or in person), then procedures can be established that will exclude all other messages during periods of time when important issues are being worked on. Noncrisis phone messages can be taken based on the fact that the decision maker is unavailable. Subordinates can be asked to come back another time. If, to avoid interruption, the decision maker must work in another office, or work at home, so be it. Unless they are of a crisis nature, the messages and people can wait — but what cannot wait is attention to those items that have been identified as having top priority. The aim of this isolation is to allow the decision maker to work on his or her list of priorities, not on priorities set by others who come with, or call in, messages.

Information Gathering. Step two, which begins after Gresham's Law of Planning has been overcome, involves an information-gathering process — a process by which one assesses the environment within which the institution operates. In promoting federal and state interests, one has to look at two major components in assessing the environment. On the one hand, one needs to gain as great an understanding as possible of what those federal and state interests are, particularly those interests that the federal government and/or the state government have stated ought to be implemented through local initiative. In short, one needs to do homework regarding what programs and services could conceivably be implemented. To this end, one obviously needs to review official publications, including: congressional actions, requests for proposals, regulations, and speeches of federal and state officials.

To be serious about this component of information gathering, the decision maker should actively attempt to establish relationships with, and enter into dialogue with, a variety of federal and state officials. At the beginning, this dialogue might just be with a congressional aide and with the person in the state capitol who is either most approachable or most concerned about the general welfare of your institution. Later on, as a narrowing of your interest in various programs takes place, the number of people with whom personal relationships are established should be greater. After this phase of information gathering is complete, you ought to have a tentative list of federal and state programs whose philosophy and method of operation lend themselves to local implementation.

The second component of information gathering is to assess the needs of the clientele you currently serve and the clientele you might potentially serve as encompassed in your official mission. Their needs ought to dictate the priorities you will assign among the various federal and state interests. It is obvious that a state program that is to be implemented locally and that has little utility for the citizens in your locality should be ranked low in your priority listing of programs.

Prioritizing. Having put together enough time to do proper planning in step one and having gathered some basic information in step two, you can go on to step three which is to make firm decisions regarding which federal and state interests your institution should seek to implement. Here the assumption is that the potential list of federal and state programs is too large for any one institution to seek to implement. A second assumption is that, no matter how much time is set aside by the decision maker and his or her staff, there is probably not enough time to generate proposals for all those programs that are accessed by grant proposals. Finally, there is an assumption that there are some federal and state interests that your institution ought not to be involved in implementing, even if there is a need on the part of your citizens for such programs. This assumption is based on recognition that you have a central mission and would not want that mission distorted by the addition of many peripheral activities. Also, there may be many other agencies within your community that either have greater expertise or, for nonpartisan political reasons, ought to be deeded the responsibility for implementing any particular federal or state interest. At the end of this step, the decision maker will have a list of federal and state programs that should be and are implemented locally, for which the institution desires to be a center of action.

Mobilization. The fourth step is the most difficult. It encompasses activities which seek the mandate to implement a federal and state interest and actually implement that interest in the local area. This step is the most difficult not because such mandates to implement are hard to secure, but because it takes more than a decision maker and staff to implement federal and state interests. The decision maker should be able to mobilize the efforts of many in the institution behind an attempt to expand the programmatic activities of the institution to provide greater services to current and potential constituencies.

Techniques that have utility in implementing any type of change involve an increase in service to constituents. Such techniques involve attitudes, people, information, and administrative action.

There is a need for the program development decision maker to spend the time with the rest of the top leadership of the institution to create an appropriate atmosphere. Ideally, a vision of improved service, if set forth vigorously enough, should stimulate many in the organization. This, however, may not be enough, and today's decision maker finds himself or herself able to use another attitude-oriented approach—that is, sharply calling to the attention of all that the institution either is in or will soon be facing a crisis if, in fact, mobilization does not take place. It is unfortunate that the creation of this type of climate is needed, but a vision of increased service may not suffice. For many institutions of higher education, forces are already at work that can be used by a decision maker to challenge all within the institution through an atmosphere that says: "If we do not seek to improve service, we will fall further behind."

There are two people-oriented techniques aimed at securing mandates to implement and actually to begin operations. The first technique involves the role of the decision maker as a creator of networks of ideas and people. The problems and programs that the federal and state interests deal with do not fall, for the most part, within neat organizational lines. The decision maker, to be effective, must be able to reach any place within the organization and even outside the organization to form ad hoc task forces of knowledgeable and interested people.

The second people-oriented technique that will help assure success is to use the current reward system of the institution or a reward system over and above that which the institution normally uses to provide some payoff to people within the institution if they dedicate their energies to implementing federal and state interests at a local level.

The first *information-oriented* technique is the use of indirect pressure to convince people of the importance of any particular objective. The phrase "prophet without honor in one's own country" is amply true for most institutions of higher education. Thus, an outside consultant, an advisory committee, or a blue-ribbon commission can have great utility in selling an idea. The second approach, which allows the decision maker to judge the strength of logical arguments and the depth of emotion against any proposal (so that it can be withdrawn if resistance is strong), is the use of trial balloons. This approach involves testing the waters, often by having others release the idea while the decision maker stands aside to judge carefully the nature of any resistance.

There are two *administrative-oriented* techniques to which attention should be called. Setting new objectives and implementing programs often fail because of administrative ineptness. A simple but highly effective approach, often violated, is to set forth a timetable for the accomplishment of tasks and simply to require that everyone adhere to the timetable. The second approach is for the decision maker to play the same role relative to those lower in the institutional hierarchy that the federal or state government is playing relative to local agencies — that is, the decision maker should set the direction, give assignments or mandates, and insist upon accountability. This approach provides flexibility and implementation by those lower in the hierarchy and draws upon the same principles of the utility of local knowledge and initiative that make it wise for federal and state interests to be implemented at the lowest level possible.

The use of these techniques obviously will not guarantee the successful receipt of mandates and their implementation. But close attention needs to be paid to mobilization through attitude creation, network creation, rewards, outside pressure, gauging of resistance, seeking of closure, and decentralization.

There is, however, another dimension of institutional response to implementing federal and state interests. This other dimension deals with the need for local agencies and institutions to influence the substance of federal and state interests.

Shaping Federal and State Interests

One of the most important aspects of our political system is the concept of lobbying. The concept can only have meaning in a political system that is open to and will tolerate the input of ideas and information. Clearly, lobbying is not devious, sleazy, or unethical. To the extent that there are federal and state interests and to the extent that those interests in many cases can best be implemented at the local level, then we have an admission that the insights and abilities of people at the local level are significant for success.

The logical extension of this is that not only are local interests important in implementation but they are also important in *setting* the original federal and state goals to which the local interests are responding. Local institutions must make input individually and collectively on an active basis to a wide variety of federal and state officials and agencies on a wide variety of issues. This input must flow from local institutions' assessments of constituent needs, the evaluation by local institutions of how well current programs are working, and local institutions' forecasts of what needs there will be in the future.

Lobbying brings up again the issue of time on the part of local decision makers, which can be translated easily into cost. It is time-consuming and costly to lobby. Also, there are immediate pressing details, perhaps more closely tied into the reward system for the local decision maker, that lead to a tendency not to become involved actively at the federal and state levels. There are also national and statewide bodies that lobby on behalf of local institutions; the existence of these groups makes it easy for local decision makers to be lulled into believing their interests are being represented adequately. Often it is the case that, for the institution that aggressively wants to secure mandates to implement federal and state interests and that organizes and mobilizes itself well internally, the picture can only be complete when that institution, singly or collectively, helps to shape the nature of federal and state interests.

For example, one area where lobbying is needed on a particular federal and state interest that has been implemented locally is federal vocational education, we have as good an example as any of local institution interest in vocational education for decades is amply proven by federal appropriations during this period. That the federal government has acknowledged a state interest in vocational education is proven by the requirement that states develop a state plan for vocational education and distribute the money to local institutions. One could argue that, in vocational education, we have as good an example an any of local institutions carrying out a federal and state interest. Indeed, most institutions offering some prebaccalaureate programs of instruction in occupational areas have planned for and sought a mandate to be an implementor of this particular federal and state interest.

For postsecondary institutions that have participated to date, it is clear that the federal and state interest has in fact encouraged, for the country as a whole, secondary vocational education at the expense of other types of postsecondary education. The major reason for this situation (other than political pressure) has been a less-than-adequate understanding on the part of the federal government regarding the changing demographics of this country. The aging of our population, particularly when taken into consideration with the degree of technological change, cries out for increased funding for postsecondary as opposed to secondary schooling. In every federal congressional session, major acts like the Vocational Education Act need intense, partisan, and complex reauthorization and campaigns. Unless local input is made to those at the federal and state level who can influence the shape of the federal legislation, much wisdom is lost.

Having just cited an area in which lobbying at the federal level is needed, we can now present three New Jersey illustrations where aggressive lobbying not only brought to the local educational institutions the mandate to implement activities but also helped shape those activities. The three illustrations concern services to the deaf community, customized training of potential employees of firms moving into New Jersey, and service to the New Jersey Department of Transportation.

In all three cases, there were needs identified by state government. In the case of service to the deaf community, state recognition of this need was manifested by the establishment of a new state division of the deaf. In the case of customized training, it was a legislative appropriation, and, in the case of service to the state department of transportation, it was a theme discussed by a new commissioner who asked for closer ties with the academic community. In all cases, the state interest was rather broad, and the method of implementation was left vague at first.

In the case of services to the deaf, today there is a new degree program to educate interpreters, and the field offices of the new division are located at three colleges. In the case of customized training, the community colleges were designated as the prime coordinators of all such training. In the case of service to the state department of transportation, many of the state colleges and universities signed general agreements with the department of transportation that facilitate the flow of specific contracts. In all three cases, active and aggressive leadership was displayed by the colleges, resulting both in their receiving a mandate and in their shaping that mandate.

Conclusion

There are certain hypotheses that have been explicitly or implicitly dealt with in this chapter.
   1. General principles from political science, economics, and business argue that local implementation is critical to the

effective implementation of federal and state interests. These principles are now being expressed in a philosophical drift toward more implementation at the local level.

2. Campus-based administrators cannot assume that, without major effort, their institutions will be effective in securing mandates to implement federal and state interests, nor can they assume that they will be successful in implementing those interests.

3. There is a process that local decision makers should experience to maximize the potential for success. This four-step process involves consideration of a number of techniques that can help mobilize institutional resources.

4. It is not enough for a local institution to be a passive recipient of what others determine to be federal and state interests. The institutions must engage in lobbying to shape those interests.

5. If such lobbying does not take place, one can assume an ineptness in defining those federal and state issues that will not be overcome no matter how brilliantly those interests are implemented.

References

Catalogue of Federal Domestic Service. Washington, D.C.: Government Printing Office, 1983.

Drucker, P. F. "Managing for Business Effectiveness." *Harvard Business Review,* 1963, *41,* 53–60.

Freedman, A. M. "Gresham's Law." In Douglas Greenwald (Ed.), *Encyclopedia of Economics.* New York: McGraw-Hill, 1982.

Juran, J. M. *Managerial Breakthrough.* New York: McGraw-Hill, 1965.

Longenecker, J. G. *Principles of Management and Organizational Behavior.* Columbus, Ohio: Merrill, 1973.

March, J. C., and Simon, H. A. *Organizations.* New York: Wiley, 1958.

Smith, A. *The Wealth of Nations.* New York: Random House, 1937 (originally published 1776).

Edward D. Goldberg, assistant chancellor for Academic Affairs in the New Jersey State Department of Higher Education, was state director of community colleges in New Jersey for over four years.

Even when concentrating on local community-organized
group interests in and need for educational services, educators
need to know the larger social and economic context.

Determining Priorities for Adult Education: An Example of Statewide Needs Assessment

Dan E. Moore

The first song in Meredith Wilson's hit muscial, *The Music Man,* ends with the phrase, "You've gotta know the territory." Getting to know the territory is one of the first steps in having a successful educational program. And no one knows this better than professionals involved in community-based postsecondary and adult education. However, systematically assessing the educational needs and program potential in a particular community or locality is no easy task. The purpose of this chapter is to describe in some detail one example of a community needs assessment—a recent statewide study of community needs conducted in Pennsylvania. In addition, findings from this Pennsylvania study that relate to educational programming will be presented briefly.

Today "needs assessment" is a popular topic in many circles, but it has a variety of meanings. Federal and state programs gave great impetus to the idea by mandating a number of needs assessments as requirements for funding. Yet in a comprehensive review of a number of state and federal programs, Kimmel (1977, p. 17) concluded that "not a single program defined needs assessment. Most of the programs state no techniques at all for conducting a needs assessment."

S. V. Martorana, W. E. Piland (Eds.). *Designing Programs for Community Groups.*
New Directions for Community Colleges, no. 45. San Francisco: Jossey-Bass, March 1984.

Although the process is generally ill-defined, its place in education is an old and important one. In fact, most of us have been conducting needs assessments of one sort or another all of our professional lives. One way is simply to keep alert to what is going on in the community: Read the local newspaper; listen carefully at gathering places such as barbershops, beauty shops, or diners; talk to students and potential students; and join a variety of social and professional clubs. If you make it known that you and your organization are open to suggestions and innovations, people will often volunteer ideas. Another way of performing informal needs assessment is by seeking out information that is already available in communities in the form of existing written materials; demographic data are provided by the U.S. Census Bureau, and a variety of social indicators are collected by national, state, and local organizations.

Caffarella (1981) distinguishes more than a dozen different definable techniques for needs assessment in addition to those just mentioned. She includes group meetings, conferences and workshops, public hearings, consultations with key informants, and participant and unobtrusive observation. One of the more formal ways of going about conducting a needs assessment is to do a survey. Yet a survey can be as extensive as a statewide study or as brief and superficial as a checklist on a postcard sent to a small number of organizations.

There is probably no one best way to conduct a needs assessment; however, there are benefits and limitations to each approach. For example, the more informal, face-to-face discussions help us to answer the questions "What?" and "Why?" We can probe for an elaboration of ideas. We can seek to understand the rationales people have for their opinions and from whom else they have heard these opinions.

The more formal survey approach, however, is probably better at answering the questions "Who?" and "How many?" For example, how extensively are the ideas and beliefs held among a more general population of organizations or people? To whom have we been speaking—only the most vocal or articulate, the most highly educated, or those who already control the most resources? Perhaps the best and most thorough strategy is to develop a needs assessment *process* that combines elements of all approaches.

Purposes of Needs Assessment

There is substantial literature on needs assessment in higher and continuing education. If you are interested in examining an array of studies done for particular colleges, the various Educational Resources

VRJC LIBRARY

Information Center (ERIC) Clearinghouses are a useful place to start. For example, Dzierlenga (1981) gives a brief annotated discussion of eight recent studies retrieved from this source. The sheer number and variety of studies make synthesizing all the material difficult. In 1979, the Office of Lifelong Learning of the Ohio Board of Regents took a novel approach to this problem (Johnson, 1980). They held the "Regents' National Competition on Assessing the Needs of Adult Learners" to identify exemplary studies. The chief characteristic of current assessment efforts, according to the sponsors of this competition, was diversity — diversity of subjects studied, of materials used, and of sponsorship.

In addition to picking exemplary studies, the sponsors commissioned K. Patricia Cross to draw on her existing work (Cross, 1979) in order to develop a chapter on the state of the art in needs assessment (Cross, 1980). Cross identifies three major purposes of past assessment studies: (1) to gauge the size and interest of potential educational markets; (2) to assess the access of various target groups to educational programs; and (3) to gain basic insight into the learning processes and preferences of learners (in this case, adult learners). Past research has generated a lot of information about these issues, but, all too often, new studies are unable to make effective use of this larger body of literature because the studies' purposes were not clearly defined. There has been a tendency to adopt someone else's approach (including someone else's questionnaire). This creates two problems: first, the study generates answers that are already known, and, second, it generates answers to questions that you or your institution never asked or wanted to know about. The bottom line is that anyone who begins a needs assessment project must spend time clarifying the information needs of their organization.

If people performing the assessment do not understand the use to which the information is to be put, they are likely to ask questions the public is unable or unwilling to answer. For example, it is probably inappropriate to ask the public for solutions to the curricular dilemmas of continuing education; however, the public *is* the single best source for specific information that will permit educators and planners to develop effective curricular solutions. To get this information, the educators must frame questions both that the public is capable of answering and that provide useful information for the decision-making process (Dillman, 1977).

One example from another realm of public policy describes a state energy planner who scoffed at the idea of a public survey assisting in solving the national energy crisis, a crisis that he viewed as highly complex and international in scope. But he did see the relevance to his work in knowing how many people were using wood stoves and how many had increased the insulation in their homes. Needs assessment researchers must be sensitive both to what the sponsoring organization wants to know and what the public is able to provide.

If, as Cross (1980) says, the major problem is to have the goals and information needs clearly defined, the next most bothersome issues are "how to convert the data into workable education programs and how to gain acceptance in the community" (p. 16). All too often, doing a needs assessment is seen as a four-step linear process: (1) a needs assessment is conducted; (2) a program is developed; (3) the program is implemented; and (4) an evaluation is conducted. A more useful approach is to view the needs assessment process as a continuous and interactive one. For example, an assessment can become an evaluation of previous programs. Existing programs are continually being changed as they are being implemented. The key element is to plan for this continuous process. Educators, community organizations, and users, whether individuals or groups, need to be involved at each step and to be flexible about moving among the steps.

More specifically, when the needs assessment is going to be a formal survey, the various constituent groups need to be actively involved in defining objectives, reacting to specific sample questions, helping to respond to the pretest instrument, and assisting in interpreting the results. Frequently educators and others who use needs assessment make the fallacious assumption that, once the answers to the questions are compiled, the policy and program directions will be obvious. This is seldom the case. The fact that the relevant groups are working cooperatively and continuously is probably as important as the answers to specific questions from the survey.

The failure to address the questions of purpose and process could be attributed to an excessive fascination with methodological niceties, such as drawing a sophisticated sample, using questions with the highest coefficients of reliability, and so on. The actual conduct of any particular needs assessment is always some balance or compromise among the issues of costs, information needs, sample size, and urgency. However, there is no reason to sacrifice rigor for usable knowledge; in fact, the two go hand in hand.

"Pennsylvania: The Citizens' Viewpoint"

Let us now turn to a consideration of "Pennsylvania: The Citizens' Viewpoint" (Moore and Ishler, 1980) as one example of a needs assessment process that attempted to take the issues we have mentioned into account. While this study does not address solely educational issues, its findings do relate to some important aspects of educational planning. The study was developed at Pennsylvania State University (Penn State) for the Cooperative Extension Service. In contrast with studies that are tightly focused on a single problem, this study had multiple objectives, some of which were quite broad in scope, yet the following goals were clearly defined:

1. Develop priorities for educational programs and program areas for the Cooperative Extension Service, particularly in the areas of community development.
2. Develop a range of information on citizens' preferences for state and local community policies in the 1980s.
3. Use the opportunity of the survey to gather information on citizen characteristics and behaviors to inform basic research in the areas of migration, energy behavior, and community service demands.

Obviously these objectives overlap to some extent, but the major criteria for including items in the survey was whether the information was seen as useful by at least one of the following groups: educators at Pennsylvania State University, public decision makers in various offices throughout the state, and researchers.

The first objective of the planners was to define the broad purposes of the study and then to decide on specific methods. Because we wanted the information to be used by state, regional, and local decision makers, it was decided that the sample size should be large enough to permit generalizations about adults residing in relatively limited local areas. Specifically, we wanted to generalize the findings to each of the sixty-seven counties in Pennsylvania. In order to address such a large and geographically diverse sample of people, we selected a mail survey as the vehicle. A number of other states have conducted similar surveys in recent years so that several models for conducting a statewide survey were available (Wardwell and Dillman, 1975; Burdge and others, 1978; Beaulieu and Korsching, 1979).

The basic objectives and the survey parameters were established in consultation with an advisory committee drawn from throughout the university. The decision was made early by the advisory committee to seek funding for the study solely from within the university so that the critical decisions would remain within the control of the survey group and outside of various political arenas. A variety of departments, institutions, colleges, and university administrators were approached about participating. While there was no promise of a direct correlation between investment and return, the general understanding was that a financial investment in the study would permit the sponsor to ask a limited number of questions within the broad objectives outlined. Sufficient funding was collected in this manner, and each of the sponsors was invited to participate on the advisory committee with a number of research and extension specialists (Moore and Ishler, 1980).

Next, in order to ensure that the information would be useful to decision makers in the state, we conducted more than 100 interviews with legislators, cabinet officials, local government officials, leaders of civic groups, and staff and advisory members of the Cooperative Extension Service. The purpose of the surveying was explained. Each interviewee was then given the opportunity to respond to the question, "If you could ask 20,000 Pennsylvanians five questions that would help you make decisions in the 1980s, what would you most like to know?" Each of the individuals contacted was enthusiastic about participating (especially after we explained that the survey would not cost them anything and was being conducted by Penn State as a part of its public service mission). Interviewees responded during the interview and were also given a simple two-page questionnaire with which to communicate additional thoughts.

Not only were these decision makers and potential users of the results important in developing ideas for the survey but also the interviews themselves marked the beginning of a process, a relationship, between the university and a number of organizations. In short, we were developing an audience for the results before the study was conducted. Throughout the entire project, we were demonstrating that our organization, the university, could cooperate and would deliver. The 100 individuals and groups were contacted for information before the questionnaire was constructed and were also involved in reviewing each draft of the questionnaire. They were kept informed at each stage of the data collection process and were the first to receive results. These individuals and organizations were key actors in the dissemination and use of the survey information.

The Survey Methodology. Cross (1980) criticizes some of the existing studies for their narrow-minded attention to methods to the exclusion of a concern for purpose and application. However, our experience is that potential data users are invariably interested in the methodology, particularly if the results do not confirm their suspicions from past experience. Put briefly, the best available methodology should be used; this means paying close attention to sample selection, instrument design, and data collection procedures.

Selecting the sample is dependent first of all on the purposes of the study. Obviously, if the goal is to understand the experiences of current or past students, such students should be the target of the needs assessment. If, as Eskow suggests at the outset in this volume, the interest is in community associations and organizations, then start with the universe of such groups, or ask individuals about their associational affiliations or other relevant characteristics that may be used as the basis for forming groups. In the Penn State citizens' survey, the objective was to draw conclusions about the general population of adults in Pennsylvania; hence, a sample from that population was our target.

In every case, it is necessary to specify the universe of all persons or organizations under study. Depending upon the length of this list and the resources available, you may need to draw a sample. Although the problem of defining and enumerating each of the elements in the universe (or the "sampling frame") is not unique to a general population survey, the problem in particularly acute for a study like the Citizens' Viewpoint. There is simply no complete list of all the adults in an area the size of a state. Some communities within a state may have such lists, but there is always the problem of how up to date the lists are and how many communities have them. There are some general sources, such as voter registration lists, telephone books, or driver's license lists; each source has its merits and limitations.

The list of licensed drivers in Pennsylvania was selected for the Citizens' Viewpoint survey for a number of reasons. First, the list is available for use by researchers. (This is not the case in all states.) Second, the list is constantly updated. (This is also not the case in all states.) Third, because the list was available for analysis before the sample was selected, we could examine its biases with respect to known characteristics of the sampling frame. On the basis of this knowledge, we could select a random sample stratified by county, age, and sex, which reflected general population parameters. In addition, the driver's license list permitted us to sample individuals and not households (which is generally the case with telephone directories).

Concerns about sampling cannot be overrated. On the other hand, it is important to recognize the potential limitations in generalizing from any sample to some larger population. There is nothing inherently wrong if the researcher takes every tenth person who passes by in a shopping center; however, everyone from the researcher to the user of the data must be cognizant of the population to which the data can be generalized. In this case, that population would be the people who pass by in a particular shopping center, not the general population of the community. The Citizens' Viewpoint survey sample was determined to be 20,000 adult citizens in the state. The driver's license list was selected as the best universe from which to produce such a sample.

Once the sample was selected, the next step was to develop a method for securing the highest response rate possible. In order to do this, we adopted the procedures described in Dillman's (1978) book on his total design method. We believe this is the best treatment of the design and conduct of a mail survey. The book also has a detailed discussion of telephone survey methods. Dillman synthesizes previous mail survey research by illustrating why one should do everything possible to decrease the cost and increase the rewards of responding for each potential respondent. He shows the importance of a cover letter that contains a carefully worded appeal and that is personally addressed and personally signed. Dillman also stresses the importance of a careful strategy of follow-up mailings.

In the Citizens' Viewpoint survey, the latest computer technology was used to personalize each of the 20,000 cover letters, to update lists of returned questionnaires, and to prepare follow-up mailings. The first mailing of the survey was sent in January 1980. A week later a follow-up postcard was sent to each of the 20,000 persons sampled, thanking them if they had responded and encouraging them to respond if they had not. Three weeks later each nonrespondent was sent a new cover letter along with a replacement questionnaire. At the end of three more weeks, those who still had not returned a questionnaire were sent a final letter and replacement questionnaire by certified mail.

The construction of the questionnaire itself is a key element in eliciting a high response rate and in obtaining quality information. Dillman spends a great deal of time elaborating alternative question formats and overall questionnaire layout. Making the questionnaire easy to read and simple to fill out is essential to reduce the "cost" to the respondent.

If there is a single key element to the success of any survey, it is the careful pretesting of the survey instruments. Following Dillman's prescription, we pretested with three distinct groups. First, we got the reactions of fellow researchers and other experts in research methods and in the substantive policy areas to be studied. These people helped make the wording of questions compatible with previous research and helped avoid errors of fact and technique. A second group included in the pretest were potential users of the research information such as government officials. In this case the pretesters interviewed earlier were used. They were helpful in assuring that the questionnaire responded to their data needs.

A third group of pretesters consisted of a sample of the general population living close to the university. These people were chosen to simulate actual respondents. Some were mailed the questionnaire; others were asked to fill out the questionnaire in the presence of the researchers so that we could have their immediate feedback.

The pretest process was interactive: Once feedback was received, a new draft of the questionnaire was developed and then subjected to further pretesting. The final questionnaire went through eight complete drafts before final printing. The questionnaire was not short; it consisted of ten pages, over 200 questions, and required approximately thirty minutes to fill out.

All of this detail may seem symptomatic of the excessive fascination with methods pointed out by Cross (1980). It is fair to ask if such detail is necessary. While we believe Cross is quite correct to say that, if details get in the way of the larger goals of clearly defining purposes and establishing processes for use, then this concern is misplaced. But the best-conceived study is virtually useless unless carefully conducted. "Garbage in, garbage out" applies to survey questionnaires as well as to using computers.

In the Citizens' Viewpoint study, over 73 percent of the sample who received questionnaires returned them in usable form. Response rate is not the only indicator of quality, but the high response rate we received does suggest that the questionnaire was relevant to the concerns of many respondents, that it was easy for the respondents to understand and return, and that the attention paid to detail helped make the study important to the respondents.

Moreover, response rate is not only a general indicator of survey quality but it is also important in itself. Our preliminary analyses of the survey responses suggest that people who respond early to mail surveys are different from those who respond late. For example, early respondents are more likely to be older, to be employed, to own their own home, and to be more conservative on a range of social policy issues than are those who respond to later mailings. If we had been satisfied with only a 30 or 40 percent response rate, we might have drawn very misleading conclusions about the population as a whole. Carefully following Dillman's total design method virtually assured us of at least a 60 percent response rate with a general population. Dillman reports response rates of over 90 percent for studies of more limited, homogeneous audiences, such as professional educators.

Some view the procedures and the total design method as too costly. However, survey researchers and particularly needs assessors cannot afford *not* to use them. Obviously, conducting needs assessment studies requires the art of compromise, but it is better to use a smaller sample and more thorough follow-up than a larger sample with no follow-up. You may end up with just as many people, but in the former case the people are a better representation of the universe under study.

Uses of the Citizens' Viewpoint Data. The amount of information generated when over 14,000 individuals complete a ten-page questionnaire is almost overwhelming. It was only because a systematic plan had been developed in line with the study objectives that it was possible to use this information in a timely manner. The first publication was a sixteen-page tabloid that summarized the statewide results for most of the questions in the survey (Moore and Ishler, 1980). The intent with this popularized format was to produce the results quickly for respondents (who were promised results if they desired), for sponsors, and for those users who were interviewed to develop the questions. The three-color tabloid also served as an advertising piece for potential users of the data base. This publication was in print less than one month after the last questionnaire was returned. The release of the tabloid with press releases and press conferences generated wide interest in the printed and electronic media throughout Pennsylvania.

As we noted earlier, the first project was to help develop program priorities for educational programs in the Cooperative Extension Service in Pennsylvania. To this end, we worked closely with state, regional, and county staff to frame questions and to produce usable reports. In addition, a set of regional publications was targeted for extension lay advisory planning committees. We also produced a ten-minute slide and audio show that was used to introduce the study to new audiences. Twelve copies of the presentation were made available to extension staff members throughout the state. By conservative estimate, more than 20,000 people saw this presentation alone. The data and reports in various forms have been used by program planning committees at all levels.

The second objective was to provide current information on public policy issues to decision makers at state and local levels. In addition to the tabloid and a variety of workshops, special reports were prepared to users' specifications. For example, the state department on aging was interested in priorities for senior citizens' services as indicated by the elderly themselves compared to the rest of the population; further, the department was interested in the differences between rural elderly and the urban elderly. We were able to use our extensive data base to produce a report that answered their specific policy questions. The initial users and requesters of special reports were the organizations interviewed to elicit questions, but a number of other organizations throughout the state also requested special reports. In all, more than 200 such publications tailored to user needs were produced in the year following the survey.

A variety of research papers has also been written based on the data set. These cover such topics as "Energy Conservation Behaviors of Different Population Segments," "Community Service Priorities of

Recent Migrants to Rural Areas," "Characteristics of Community Political Activists and Their Modes of Community Participation," and "An Analysis of Public Acceptance of Alternative Taxing Schemes for Public Education." Future plans call for merging the survey data with the results of the 1980 census when those data become available. Since the data from both sources were collected contemporaneously, we believe the merger of selected variables will produce some interesting new insights.

Priorities for Educational Programs:
An Example from the Citizens' Viewpoint Survey

To illustrate the type of questions asked in the survey, we provide here a set of six items pertaining to education. One overall question posed by the survey was, "Compared to what is being done now, what priority do you want the following areas to have in the future?" Respondents were asked to choose among "much lower," "lower," "same," "higher," and "much higher" for each of forty-nine community services and issues ranging from garbage collection to teenage drug and alcohol abuse.

None of the six educational items ranked among the top ten of the forty-nine. The top spots were held by items pertaining to citizen-government relations: road repair, and jobs (Moore and Ishler, 1980). The results for the six educational items are presented in Tables 1 and 2. The far right column of Table 1 suggests that 62 percent of all respondents felt that vocational and technical education programs should have a "higher" or "much higher" priority in the future. The only other educational item where at least half of the adult population selected these alternatives for a higher priority was adult and continuing education. The more traditional educational institutions and programs do not require as much attention according to our respondents. A glance across the rows of Table 1 will show that the priorities are relatively consistent by age of respondent. Generally the age group from twenty-five to forty-four expressed the highest level of concern for each of the educational programs.

Table 2 presents the same educational items by the educational level of the respondent. The results provide an interesting counterpoint to the standard finding that the more education people have, the more interest they have in more education (Cross, 1980). While we did not specifically ask people if they themselves wanted more education, there is no consistent pattern in Table 2 about educational priorities by the educational level of the respondent. In fact, in none of the six areas

Table 1. Priorities for Educational Programs by Age

	Age of Respondent				
Educational Programs	18–24	25–44	45–60	61 and Over	All Respondents
Elementary Schools	33[a]	41	29	30	34
Junior and Senior High Schools	38	42	30	30	36
Vocational, Technical	61	66	60	57	62
Community Colleges	35	37	33	27	34
Colleges, Universities	35	32	25	22	29
Adult and Continuing	58	54	46	41	50
Approximate Sample Size[b]	1626	3388	2578	2020	9957

[a] Figures represent the percent of respondents indicating a "higher" or "much higher" priority for the item.
[b] The column totals do not add to the total number of respondents because of missing data for some of the items.

does the group having the highest education also have the highest aggregate priority for educational programs. Indeed, in virtually every case, the group with the least education gives the educational items as high a priority as the college-educated group.

Table 2. Priorities for Educational Programs by Education Level of Respondent

	Education of Respondents				
Educational Programs	Less Than High School Graduate	High School Graduate	Some College	College Graduate	All Respondents
Elementary Schools	34[a]	35	34	33	34
Junior and Senior High Schools	34	36	38	35	36
Vocational, Technical	61	63	64	57	62
Community Colleges	30	34	39	30	34
Colleges, Universities,	25	27	32	31	29
Adult and Continuing	47	48	54	49	50
Approximate Sample Size[b]	1790	3405	2596	2018	9957

[a] Figures represent the percent of respondents indicating a "higher" or "much higher" priority for the item.
[b] The column totals do not add to the total number of respondents because of missing data for some of the items.

Of what use are these data? The findings confirm the suspicions of those involved in education at all levels. Pennsylvania citizens reflect the national trend toward more emphasis on vocational, technical, and adult continuing education and toward a decrease in the overall ranking of education among the priorities of citizens. These findings raise further questions, however, about how sex, group affiliations, and occupational status relate to the various priority choices indicated. The large sample size of the Citizens' Viewpoint survey permits this kind of detailed exploration of questions that may emerge in policy discussions.

Conclusion

The Citizens' Viewpoint study illustrates clearly the three main points in Cross's (1980) brief review of the needs assessment literature: Any study must have a set of carefully delineated objectives; it should be seen as a part of a continuing planning process; and it should use the state of the art in survey methodology. Because of the purposefully broad objectives of the Citizens' Viewpoint survey, a significant strength of the study was the ability to make comparisons among broad policy priorities in a number of substantive areas. On the other hand, it was difficult to examine any particular area in the depth or detail that a single-focus, targeted study would be able to do.

It is important to realize that seldom will the results of the needs assessment or a citizen survey definitively decide policy questions, but such work can provide important and timely information to a decision maker. The context and clientele of decisions can be more fully elaborated. Finally, the needs assessment activity can set in motion a process of continuing discussion among various actors in the policy-making arena, whether it be education, local government, or voluntary associations.

References

Beaulieu, J., and Korsching, P. P. (Eds.). *Focus on Florida: The Citizens' Viewpoint.* Special Series No. 1. Center for Community and Rural Development—Institute for Food and Agriculture Science. Gainesville: University of Florida, May 1979.

Burdge, J., Kelly, R. M., and Schweitzer, H. J. *Illinois: Today and Tomorrow.* Cooperative Extension Publication, Special Series No. 1, Urbana, Ill.: College of Agriculture, University of Illinois, 1978.

Caffarella, R. S. *Needs Assessment.* Diffusion of Innovations Handbook Series. Orono: College of Education of Maine, 1981.

Cross, K. P. "A Critical Review of State and National Studies of the Needs and Interests of Adult Learners." In C. B. Stalford (Ed.), *Adult Learning Needs and the Future Demand for Lifelong Learning.* Washington, D.C.: National Institute of Education, 1979.

84

Cross, K. P. "The State of the Art in Needs Assessment." In L. G. Johnson (Ed.), *Assessing the Needs of Adult Learners: Methods and Models.* Columbus: Ohio Board of Regents, 1980.

Dillman, D. A. "Preference Surveys and Policy Decisions: Our New Tools Need Not Be Used in the Same Old Way." *Journal of the Community Development Society,* 1977, *8* (1), 44–53.

Dillman, D. A. *Mail and Telephone Surveys: The Total Design Method.* New York: Wiley, 1978.

Dzierlenga, D. W. "Assessing Community Needs with Surveys." *Catalyst,* 1981, *11* (2), 26–29.

Johnson, L. G. (Ed.). *Assessing the Needs of Adult Learners: Methods and Models.* Columbus: Ohio Board of Regents, 1980.

Kimmel, W. A. *Needs Assessment: A Critical Perspective.* Washington, D.C.: U.S. Department of Health, Education, and Welfare, 1977.

Moore, D. E., and Ishler, A. S. "Pennsylvania: The Citizens' Viewpoint." University Park: College of Agriculture, Pennsylvania State University, 1980.

Wardwell, J. M., and Dillman, D. A. *The Alternatives for Washington Surveys: The Final Report.* Vol. 6. Olympia, Wash.: Office of Program Planning and Fiscal Management, 1975.

Dan E. Moore is associate professor of rural sociology and extension specialist at Pennsylvania State University.

Three basic questions must be confronted by each community college as it considers tackling the challenge of the new mission.

Promises and Pitfalls in Serving Organized Community-Based Group Interests

S. V. Martorana
William E. Piland

A proposed new departure for any organization or institution is always sure to cause tension and controversy both for the organization and between it and other external groups. This is likely to prove true again for community colleges and other types of community-based postsecondary educational institutions that rise to the challenge posed by Eskow in Chapter One and built upon as the main theme of this volume. Such institutions should be alert not only to the tensions and controversies sure to arise but also to the nature of the issues likely to surface and the alignments of support or challenge likely to take shape.

This brief chapter, then, raises and comments on three broad questions. Brevity, however, is dictated by more than just limitations of space in this particular publication. It is mandated in part to avoid repeating some of the observations already made by other chapter authors, but, even more important, it is forced by the paucity of relevant materials that can be drawn upon to answer the questions that can be raised. There is no significant literature on the main subject of this

S. V. Martorana, W. E. Piland (Eds.). *Designing Programs for Community Groups.*
New Directions for Community Colleges, no. 45. San Francisco: Jossey-Bass, March 1984.

volume, no body of work either based on research or reporting case experience in depth. Thus, community-based institutions will have to ask and seek answers largely on their own to these big questions:

1. Why should the new approach (Eskow's challenge) be tried?
2. What forces within the institution will tend to facilitate positive response to the challenge and which ones will generate negative conditions?
3. What forces outside of the institution will provide support for or resistance to the undertaking?

A long list of further questions emerges quickly from these three. They are, however, clearly subordinate, and one could contend that, until better understanding about the three big questions is developed from an accumulation of experience and related analytical studies, efforts to pursue more specific inquiries are premature.

Determining Reasons for New College-Community Cooperation

An attempt to answer the "Why do it at all?" question, of course, is the main thrust of Eskow's statements in Chapter One. But he makes the case for and calls for action by "the movement" at large. This makes it easy for an institution to set the question aside as being pertinent for others in the larger group but not for it as an individual member. The leadership of each community-based postsecondary institution must find positive answers to the questions of why to adopt the approach — or else nothing of meaning can be expected to follow.

In recent years, a plethora of services, programs, and specialized functions have been embraced by community colleges under the banner of "community needs" while others have duplicated the functions of existing community-based groups or agencies. At present, community colleges appear to be moving toward a redefinition of their role and mission. Shrinking or stabilized resources, tax revolts, and a shift of emphasis from increasing open access to cutting back to the basics have begun to limit the growth of community services in many community colleges. A large number of colleges appear to be questioning the need for community services or, at least, they are looking at the limits that should be placed on this broad area of a college's total educational program.

Linkages with the community and interagency cooperation seem to be a necessity for community colleges in the years ahead. The sharing of resources and dividing of functions between community colleges and other agencies or groups should add to the efficient delivery of services to groups within the local community. Indications are strong that interinstitutional cooperation based on principles of regional planning for postsecondary education is on the increase (Martorana and Nespoli, 1978; Martorana and Kuhns, 1983). Cooperative efforts ought to help community colleges maintain a viable program of community services without duplicating existing services or depleting scarce resources.

Some observers of community colleges may respond to these ideas by claiming that the individual institutions are not that autonomous in setting their own goals and developing programs related to them. In such cases, they could ask, should not the responsibility for action be placed with officials at higher levels of the organizational structure — for example, with the state directors of state systems?

The answer is yes. The record of progress of community colleges in other areas where significant breakthroughs have occurred shows how critical systemwide and state-level leadership can be. Successes in opening the door of postsecondary educational opportunity to a wider range of students, in making vocational education a legitimate part of the curriculum, and in acquiring broad acceptance of developmental studies are examples. These changes are now generally taken for granted, but efforts toward these accomplishments were at one time questioned, and systemwide and state-level leadership helped make the case for them. In doing so, however, these leaders also had to find positive answers to the question of why. Even community colleges that are part of a system of institutions operating at substate or state levels must justify major new departures on their own terms. It is unlikely that the question will get good answers without the joint effort of leadership on both group and individual levels of operation.

A state-level board or agency charged with regulating or coordinating community colleges can provide the leadership necessary for the system to serve organized interest groups. Regional planning, interinstitutional cooperative agreements, and statewide needs assessments (Cross, 1979) can all be furthered by the state community college board or agency. This type of leadership need not subvert local initiative and control. Rather it can assist and, in some instances, provide direction to local efforts.

Cooperation among community colleges often leads to an efficiency in serving organized community-based interest groups. For example, regional planning, such as is occurring in Illinois under the leadership of the Illinois Community College Board, provides for division of labor that allows community colleges in a region to capitalize on their strengths. Organized community groups that overlap community college district boundaries can be served by the college that has the resources and strength to serve that group best through a regional cooperative agreement or through a regionwide plan. With this arrangement, artificial barriers and intercollege warfare are eliminated, and a group is served — not caught in the middle of a jurisdictional dispute.

Furthermore, the state community college board or agency can initiate, or at least assist in, forming cooperative arrangements with other governmental agencies to help individual community colleges respond to local groups. State, county, and municipal or local government agencies can help or hinder our colleges in serving their constituents. At the state level, the various code departments, commissions, councils, and agencies may already have working relationships with community groups. Numerous interactions between the colleges and these state entities are often possible. And these interactions can lead to the provision of better services to members of organized interest groups. Recently, the Illinois Community College Trustees Association sponsored the development of a *State Agency Guide* (Piland and Shade, 1982) for use by the state's community colleges to help identify, understand, and use the various state agencies that have an impact on community groups.

Of course, what is true at the state level is perhaps even more true at the local level. Here, governmental agencies and bodies often have an immediate and persuasive impact on community college interactions with community groups. Nevertheless, the state board or agency can provide the leadership in getting the local government entity and the community college working together to meet group needs. One example of this type of cooperation occurred when the Arizona Community College Board, the mayor's office of one of the cities, and the local community college worked together to help an industrial firm relocate to an Arizona city (Boyd-Beauman and Piland, 1983). Another example is presented in the chapter in this volume by Borgen and Shade; the important local, organized, special-interest group in the case they describe was a chamber of commerce.

Identifying Supporters and Resisters Within the Institution

Within the institution, the proposition that community colleges can and should develop programs and services to meet the needs of *organized* community groups will find quickly both strong support and intense opposition. Hyland in Chapter Three properly warns of the risks advocates of the idea will run. During the past year we have deliberately used several opportunities to raise the proposition in meetings with groups of faculty and administrators of community colleges and other types of community-based institutions. The nature of the discussions that followed reinforced our expectations about reactions and alignments.

Reactions in support of as well as in opposition to the idea came from all sectors of faculty (liberal arts and sciences as well as occupational). Positions taken for or against resulted apparently more from beliefs about the institution's mission and questions of feasibility of implementing the new approach than from fields of academic specialization.

Proponents of the idea see in it a new realm of academic service consistent with the philosophy and goals of a comprehensive community-based college. Some see the opportunity for enrollment increases and consequent better justification for fiscal support of programs offered; few community college faculty can forget that most colleges are financed according to formulas resting on the numbers of full-time equivalent (FTE) students enrolled. This self-enhancing view, however, is quickly dampened by funding realities across the nation. Some state legislatures are caught up in the rhetoric of "downsizing" higher and postsecondary education. While funding may be tied to full-time credit hours generated (FTEs), the size of the appropriation is, in some cases, declining in real dollars. The money behind each FTE or credit hour thereby decreases when credits or FTEs increase. Serving community interest groups by linking with other community-based agencies, as described in Hyland's chapter, can become a cost-effective way of meeting needs, whether or not credits are generated in the process.

Resisters of the proposed approach also express quite predictable reactions. One reaction is that the proposition is too risky because the interests of certain organized groups are too politically charged. An organized environmental protection group, for example, may be promoting a line of action in direct conflict with that being advocated by the board of directors of a major local industrial plant; in such a case, should the environmentalist group's interest in studying subjects related to environmental health be responded to by the local community college? How to deal with providing information and instruction while avoiding political positions on issues related to the subject taught is, of course, not a new problem in education. Faculty, as individuals and as groups responsible for the curriculum, have always dealt with that difficulty in working with individual students. Whether the same principles and practices can also be used in dealing with whole groups remains to be seen. But a test of that proposition is a function of the faculty, and their duty is to respond.

Another reaction, very much to be expected, raises questions of legitimacy on grounds other than political. What if the group's interests are exploitative, of questionable ethics, or downright criminal? Again, one versed in the academic life might well respond that the same determinations face a teacher with an individual student — except that in the latter case there is a body of experience, study, policy, and protocol that guides one to the answer. Can the same kind of resource be developed to deal with matters of service to the educational interests of people learning in groups — can we establish defensible guidelines for curriculum development to serve group purposes?

A third and, for the purpose of this discussion, last reaction reflects another expected adherence to traditional academic concepts and practices. The reaction expresses concern for the depth and quality of the educational experience provided. Such questions arise as these: How long will the "course" be? Will students want credit toward a degree or certificate? To what degree or certificate should it apply? Can the credit be transferable?

Community colleges, not too many years ago, were exciting, enterprising, and "new" educational institutions. During the past two decades, the "action" in education was in the community colleges, and it still is in many instances. In the 1960s and 1970s, though, the "people's" colleges were (1) developing flexible schedules, (2) pioneering the use of innovative institutional delivery systems, (3) taking the college to the people, and (4) expanding recruitment to citizens who never thought of attending a college. Now standard practices and tradition have begun to take hold. Faculty and administrators look askance at new ideas and at the directions (seen as "fads") that have gotten education into the mess it is in today based upon the reports of various governmental commissions and learned societies. They have therefore developed a tendency to "dig in their heels" and resist approaches that might alter the way they educate since their way has to be good because it appears to be working. Inertia is, however, the trademark of the obsolete. If the community colleges are going to serve the educational needs of their communities, they will need to balance the traditional with new programs and services. The bonds of credits, times, and traditional program structures must be loosened to accommodate the special educational needs of organized interest groups.

In summary, the pitfalls within the college into which the proposed new departure for community college program development can fall are largely ones of inertia and tradition. Opposition will come from individuals and groups within the institution that fall into two large classes: (1) ones who see no reason to change and (2) those who do not wish to have change occur because they fear or do not understand how to handle it. In today's times, the first group must make its case. The second will need help to adapt old concepts, or to develop new practices, to fit new conditions.

Looking at External Support and Resistance

For each of the sources within the college of support of or opposition to the idea of developing new connections with the community, there exist external allies. Outside the institution, however, different alignments for or against serving organized community groups can be expected. In general, sources identified as possible supporters are also advocates of strengthened community services, individuals and groups who see a community-based institution as a resource to promote all lines of community development and enrichment, not only well-established, traditional ones.

Many groups suggest, however, that these supporters may well be concentrated among the usual advocates of "opening up the system"— representatives of minorities, ethnics, labor, and so on. The implication is that more traditionally oriented external interests may be similarly concentrated on the opposing side. Characteristically, such conservative groups are particularly sensitive to concerns of the taxpayer and are more likely to defend older, more established community college programs. Of course, these traditionally conservative special-interest groups are often community-based groups with as equal a claim to the community college's educational programs and services as the more liberal groups. Too frequently, however, these conservative groups do not or cannot view the community college as a potential resource.

Yet, over the past few years, groups that historically were not community college advocates have begun using their local community college's educational programs and services. Two such examples are small business people and farmers. Because of heavy real and personal property taxes paid by these groups, they have been reluctant to support educational enterprises that increase taxes. In a recent survey of Illinois community colleges, though, these colleges reported increased services and programs for small business as a major contribution to local community economic development efforts. The colleges located in rural areas reported similar increases to farm groups (Boyd-Beauman and Piland, 1983). By establishing linkages with taxpayer groups and other seemingly hostile special-interest organizations, the community college can demonstrate its value to those groups and provide services or programs that just might become invaluable.

Taxpayer groups can be expected to challenge the use of public funds for services to "special-interest" groups, refusing to acknowledge the "public" benefit that could result. That kind of large philosophical or public policy issue can cloud or even forestall discussion of more specific minor related issues, particularly those that surround the need to finance the new approach. Finding answers to the now-hackneyed queries, "Who benefits? Who pays?" is difficult enough when only conventional proposals and approaches in postsecondary education are in mind. Breneman and Nelson (1981) correctly have alerted the field to the general lack of public policy in favor of using public funds for community services and the apparent reluctance to create such policy. Martorana and his colleagues (Martorana and Smutz, 1980; Martorana and Broomall, 1981, 1982) provide supporting evidence that state legislatures and state-level officials show little interest in changing public policies from basically traditional views. Their observations again are made largely in the context of current approaches to justifying community college programs and to current modes of financing them.

Another recently emerging nationwide concern can also get in the way of the new approach suggested here—that is, the plight of the transfer program. Voices calling for reexamination of the "community college mission" are getting louder. Interestingly, some call for a recapturing of the transfer function ("Text of the Recommendations," 1982); others suggest it should be deemphasized (Breneman and Nelson, 1981); while others simply raise the question (California Postsecondary Education Commission, 1981; Cohen and Brawer, 1982).

The point to note here is that an effort to revitalize the transfer function in community colleges could detract attention from the possibility of other new services to organized community group interests. It is possible to view both funding and institutional energy as a zero-sum game where increased attention to one function leads automatically to reduction in attention to some other one. As new attention and money go to revitalize the transfer function, will opportunity for a new kind of outlook in educational programming be lost? We all will and should cry for the needed effort to keep transfer programs alive and well; does that free us from being alert and responsive to new, useful, and desirable ways to serve?

These questions related to the transfer function are particularly perplexing. Though the importance of transfer education has been decreasing at the expense of vocational and adult education, it remains a function close to the hearts of faculty and academic area administrators as well as to sizable numbers of students. It appears that this important aspect of a community college's mission will be a volatile one in the future. While the cohort groups decrease in size, the economy, the public's interest in a college education (Fifteenth Annual Gallup Poll, 1983), the returning adult student, increasing participation rates, and numerous other variables will impact the numbers of students enrolled with transfer as their goal. In some instances, serving community-based groups and the transfer function need not be mutually exclusive. The courses that comprise a student's transfer program are frequently courses that fulfill general education requirements. Individual members of special-interest groups can and do enroll in general education courses (Willett, 1982). Educating internal constituent groups to this possibility can reduce the volume of discourse about resource-sapping efforts when attempting to meet special-interest group needs.

Conclusion

Questions like those mentioned in this chapter should be raised and attempts made to answer them. An intent to stimulate that kind of discussion is one reason for producing this sourcebook. An even more ambitious reason is the hope that the discussion will lead to some new breakthroughs and actions that speak more directly to the same issues. We need more know-how about identifying organized community groups, finding out how education can enhance their interests, formulating appropriate educational programs to do that, and evaluating results of what comes out. Some community colleges have made progress in these areas by utilizing the marketing concept. As Myran and Ralph (1981) have stated, "The future of the community college will be shaped by the scope and quality of the interactions it creates with the wide range of community groups that use its services or provide financial and political support" (p. 114). A sound marketing strategy can help community colleges learn about and reach out to community groups. Said another way, we need analysts and researchers as well as program directors and developers in the new field. Most of all, we need more attention to the potential it holds for making the American pluralistic social order, which is clearly valued in our nation, work better.

References

Boyd-Beauman, F., and Piland, W. E. *Economic Development Efforts in Community Colleges.* Normal: Center for Higher Education, Illinois State University, 1983.

Breneman, D., and Nelson, S. C. *Financing Public Community Colleges: An Economic Perspective.* Washington, D.C.: Brookings Institute, 1981.

94

California Postsecondary Education Commission. *Missions and Functions of the California Community Colleges.* Commission Report 81–14. Sacramento: California Postsecondary Education Commission, 1981.

Cohen, A. M., and Brawer, F. B. *The American Community College.* San Francisco: Jossey-Bass, 1982.

Cross, K. P. "A Critical Review of State and National Studies of the Needs and Interests of Adult Learners." In C. B. Stalford (Ed.), *Adult Learning Needs and the Future Demand for Lifelong Learning.* Washington, D.C.: National Institute of Education, 1979.

"Fifteenth Annual Gallup Poll of Public Attitudes Toward Education." *Phi Delta Kappan,* 1983, *65* (1), 33–47.

Martorana, S. V., and Nespoli, L. A. *Regionalism in American Postsecondary Education: Concepts and Practices.* University Park: Center for the Study of Higher Education, Pennsylvania State University, 1978.

Martorana, S. V., and Smutz, W. D. *State Legislation Affecting Community and Junior Colleges, 1979.* University Park: Center for the Study of Higher Education, Pennsylvania State University, 1980. Report #35.

Martorana, S. V., and Broomall, J. K. *State Legislation Affecting Community and Junior Colleges, 1980.* University Park: Center for the Study of Higher Education, Pennsylvania State University, 1981. Report #37.

Mortorana, S. V., and Broomall, J. K. *State Legislation Affecting Community, Junior, and Two-Year Technical Colleges.* University Park: Center for Study of Higher Education, Pennsylvania State University, 1982. Report #39.

Martorana, S. V., and Kuhns, E. "Cooperative Regional Planning and Action to Enhance Postsecondary Education Across State Lines." Financial Report to the Fund for the Improvement of Postsecondary Education (FIPSE), March 1983.

Myran, G., and Ralph, M. "Evaluation of Marketing Practices in Community Colleges." In W. A. Keim and M. C. Keim (Eds.), *Marketing the Program.* New Directions for Community Colleges, no. 36. San Francisco: Jossey-Bass, 1981.

Piland, W. E., and Shade, R. *State Agency Guide.* Springfield: Illinois Community College Trustees Association, 1982.

"Text of the Recommendations of the Ford Foundation's Panel." *Chronicle of Higher Education,* 1982, *23* (21), 10–14.

Willett, L. H. "Continuing Education Student Flow Analysis." *Research in Higher Education,* 1982, *17* (2), 155–164.

S. V. Martorana is a professor of higher education at Pennsylvania State University.

William E. Piland is coordinator of the Postsecondary Education doctoral degree program at Illinois State University.

The experiences of other colleges and communities working together, as documented in the literature, are helpful to community colleges embarking on this new mission.

Sources of Information: A Review of the Literature

Jim Palmer

Previous chapters have examined several aspects of the two-year college's role in serving the diverse educational needs of the community. As a resource for readers seeking further information, this final chapter reviews a selection of the documents that have been processed by the Educational Resources Information Center (ERIC) Clearinghouse for Junior Colleges since 1981. These documents deal with the community services function, community education, community development, and the involvement of the community in the college.

The Community Services Function

Community services programs have long since established themselves alongside vocational and transfer programs as a major organizational component of the two-year college. Recent ERIC documents indicate, however, that the community services segment is struggling to maintain its position of importance in the curriculum. Atwell and others (1982) argue that the community services function has not achieved its full potential because administrators have not identified the specific role to be played by the community services program

S. V. Martorana, W. E. Piland (Eds.). *Designing Programs for Community Groups.*
New Directions for Community Colleges, no. 45. San Francisco: Jossey-Bass, March 1984.

in carrying out the college's mission. As a result, the authors maintain, there is widespread disagreement as to the relative value of community services and a concomitant unwillingness of legislative bodies to fund community services programs adequately.

The difficulty of fostering strong public support for the community services function during recessionary times is illustrated in the recent struggle of the California community colleges to meet a legislatively mandated reduction in 1982–1983 state apportionments to the colleges (*Implementation of the Budget Act Language,* 1982). In order to fulfill the mandate, the state chancellor's office and the board of governors of the colleges came to the conclusion that avocational, recreational, and personal development courses that had been offered free of charge should be offered as self-supporting community services classes. The California Postsecondary Education Commission concluded that "of the three broad concepts of community college mission — baccalaureate [sic] transfer education, vocational education, and adult general education — clearly it is the last which the legislature intended to target as a low public priority" (*Implementation of the Budget Act Language,* 1982, p. 37).

Fiscal problems have led community services professionals to call for a fee-based consumer orientation in program development and delivery. Ireland and Gegna (1983) recommend that the Los Angeles Community College District create a self-supporting "Community Services Institute that would provide credit-free programs developed around a unifying theme and funded primarily by participant fees and contracts" (p. iii). Beachler (1982), in order to help administrators analyze the market for community services programs, outlines the components of a "Fiscal Trend Monitoring System" (FTMS) that utilizes demographic and economic data in market measurement and forecasting, market segmentation, and consumer analysis. The author provides an example of the use of the FTMS at the Community College of Allegheny County (Pennsylvania).

Community Education

A major function of the community services program is the provision of lifelong education at the workplace and in the community at large. This community-based education rests on the philosophy that educational needs continue throughout life, regardless of one's formal educational attainment. Furthermore, the community education program focuses on learning, rather than on degrees, credits, and credentials (Gollattscheck, 1980).

ERIC literature on this topic illustrates several approaches to the delivery of community education. These include joint efforts between colleges and local community agencies (Beachler, 1981; Jellison, 1981); the provision of on-site instruction at local businesses, agencies, and clubs (Demaris, 1980); and the use of traveling displays and booklets to involve citizens in an examination of local community history (Lieberman, 1981). One document, published by the Wisconsin State Department of Public Instruction (*An Introduction to Community Education for Wisconsin*, 1980), examines four steps in the development of community education programs: establishment of a community education steering committee; establishment of communications between the college and key community groups; recruitment of personnel to administer the community education program; and the establishment of a permanent advisory council.

While community education programs have traditionally been offered at minimal cost, colleges are now contracting customized educational services, on a profit-making basis, to local businesses and industry. Portland Community College's Institute for Community Assistance, for example, assists college staff in identifying target customers for these customized services and in contacting customers, writing up contracts for instructional services, pricing services, billing the customer, and evaluating individual programs. The institute's guidebook provides a sample contract and a tuition pricing schedule (*User's Guide to Educational Marketing*, 1981). Additional information on special community college centers that contract educational services to business, industry, and government is provided by Mahoney (1982), who draws a composite of the goals, objectives, services, linkage approaches, program development procedures, and administrative characteristics of the centers.

Community Development

Besides the provision of community education, two-year colleges are actively involved in the broader area of community development. A commitment to community development identifies the college not only as an instructional delivery system but also as a catalyst of the socio-economic well-being of the community at large. Some two-year college leaders, including Gleazer (1980), advocate a wide-ranging community development role that would involve the college and other local agencies in cooperative efforts designed to solve problems in the areas of housing, employment, nutrition, health, and other basic needs. Gleazer points out, however, that the "degree of involvement in this community development role varies, apparently, with different views of appropriateness and with respect to what the college is authorized to do under law and regulation" (p. 37).

A sociopolitical approach to community development is discussed by Hakanson (1980). Noting that a community is defined by the common interests of a group of people and that community development involves the joint efforts of these people in addressing shared problems, Hakanson maintains that the most important component of the community development process is instruction in the skills needed for effective political and social involvement. Such instruction, he continues, should be targeted toward housewives, the elderly, idealistic young people, and other persons who may have few opportunities for social contacts but who can provide the community with a heretofore untapped source of energy and insight.

Another approach to community development is the provision by the college of artistic and cultural programs that enhance the community's overall quality of life. Blackhawk College in Illinois, for example, promotes the fine arts in its rural service district by involving the citizens in a variety of activities related to drama, art, and music. Through this community arts program, 1,600 persons a year take part in such activities as a college-community choir, a college-community dinner theater, performances by touring theater groups, and exhibits of local and state artists. The program's organizational structure incorporates advisory committee members, community volunteers, and support personnel from the college (Simpson, 1982).

In contrast to these cultural and sociopolitical emphases, many two-year colleges center their community development efforts on job training. Much of the impetus for these efforts stems from the need to retrain unskilled and displaced workers in an increasingly technological economy. Indeed, Groff (1983) maintains that "human resource development, the prevention of human obsolescence, is the biggest challenge to postsecondary education in the years ahead" (p. 5).

An example of this job-training approach to community development is North Carolina's Human Resources Development (HRD) program, under which many of the state's community colleges provide unemployed citizens with remedial education, occupational training, and career guidance. State HRD appropriations are made to colleges on the basis of the degree to which the posttraining economic performance of participants is better than their pretraining performance" (*HRD Yesterday and Today*, 1982, p. 10). Because this posttraining economic performance is measured in terms of gains in earnings and reductions in public assistance, HRD funds are tied to the degree to which colleges enhance area economic viability.

An example of this job-training approach to community development is provided by Moore (1982), who describes Chemeketa (Oregon) Community College's short-term training programs. These programs focus on the acquisition of specific technical skills and deliberately minimize general education and peripheral course work. The open-entry/ open-exit, competency-based programs have been used to train dislocated workers in the areas of electronics technology, computer operations, microprocessor repair, and computer-assisted drafting.

Involving the Community in the College

In order to maintain viable community services, education, and development programs, colleges need to remain informed of community needs and to secure the input of the community in college operations. Community surveys and lay advisory committees are two mechanisms by which two-year colleges maintain close ties with local service districts.

Scores of ERIC documents describe the methodology and outcomes of community surveys that have been conducted by individual two-year colleges. Most of these surveys are designed to assess community educational needs. In conducting needs assessments, many researchers elicit opinions from a sample of the general population living within the service district (see, for example, Butler, 1981a; Clegg and Tippett, 1982; Dennis-Rounds, 1983; *Reading Area Community College,* 1981; Rosberg, 1981; and *A Survey of the Attitudes...,* 1980). Other researchers attempt to target specific subgroups of the population, such as employers, farmers, high school students, or community agencies. (Examples include *Academic Program Needs Assessment,* 1981; Arman, 1982; Moore, 1980; Muraski, 1982; Needham, 1982; Stoehr and Banerdt, 1983; Waddell and Hunt, 1982). The surveys provide the colleges with valuable information concerning: projected enrollment; preferences for the location of classes; community demand for occupational, avocational, cultural, noncredit, and other college programs; reasons why area residents do or do not enroll in college programs; learning methods that area citizens are most comfortable with; and citizen awareness of college offerings. In addition, the surveys provide data concerning demographic and other characteristics of area citizens.

Besides soliciting information concerning educational needs, community surveys are often conducted to assess citizen attitudes toward the college. Recent ERIC documents describing such surveys include Butler (1981b), Arrington and others (1979), Hastings (1982), Lau (1982), Ryan and Juba (1982), and *Taxation and Community Services* (1982). These surveys have been conducted by individual colleges to solicit opinions concerning the degree to which institutional goals are being met, citizen satisfaction with adult education programs, community problems that demand immediate attention, citizen attitudes toward the various missions of the comprehensive community college, local taxation rates, the quality of teaching at the community college, and overall citizen satisfaction with the college. Documents describing these surveys, as well as the needs assessments mentioned above, usually provide a copy of the survey instrument and describe the survey methodology.

While surveys provide a means of monitoring the population at large, advisory committees provide an avenue for citizen involvement in college operations and planning. The committees, made up of individuals with special knowledge and expertise, are usually formed to give advice on educational programs and college planning. Hagerstown Junior College (Maryland), for example, utilizes advisory committees to provide advice and counsel on the development, maintenance, operation, and modification of occupational programs; to suggest types of educational and technical services needed by the community; and to participate in program evaluation (*Hagerstown Junior College Advisory Committee Handbook*, 1982). Other examples described in the recent ERIC literature include the Lay Committee for the Humanities at the San Diego Community College District (*Citizens' Humanities Advisory Committee...*, 1983); the use of an advisory committee at Delgado Community College (Louisiana) to plan a community education needs assessment (Hopson and others, 1983); and the Black Advisory Committee formed at Valencia Community College (Florida) to monitor and assess the progress made by the college in increasing enrollment and meeting the needs of black students (*The Black Advisory Committee...*, 1980). General discussions concerning the role of advisory committees in vocational programs and in humanities programs are provided, respectively, by McQuay and Watters (1980) and by Brawer and Gates (1981).

Conclusion

A large portion of the two-year college literature is devoted to the efforts of administrators and educators to strengthen the ties between the college and the community. The items mentioned in this chapter represent only a sample of the ERIC literature on this topic. Additional information can be obtained through computer or manual searches of ERIC's *Resources in Education* (RIE) and *Current Index to Journals in Education* (CIJE). The quarterly editions of the *Community Services Catalyst*, a publication of the National Council on Community Services and Continuing Education, are another valuable resource.

The full text of the items listed under "References," unless otherwise noted, can be ordered through the ERIC Document Reproduction Service (EDRS) or obtained on microfiche at over 730 libraries across the country. For an EDRS order form and/or a list of the libraries in your state that have ERIC microfiche collections, please contact the ERIC Clearinghouse for Junior Colleges, 8118 Math-Sciences Building, University of California at Los Angeles (UCLA), Los Angeles, California 90024.

References

Academic Program Needs Assessment. Danielson, Conn.: Quinebaug Valley Community College, 1981. 14 pp. (ED 223 304)

Arman, H. D. "Community Colleges and Agricultural Education: Strategies for Serving a New Market." Paper presented at the annual conference of the National Council on Community Services and Continuing Education, Detroit, Oct. 1982. 14 pp. (ED 221 256)

Arrington, R., and others. *Community Needs Survey.* Pleasant Hill, Calif.: Diablo Valley College; San Francisco: Field Research Corporation, 1979. 78 pp. (ED 210 082)

Atwell, C. A., Vaughan, G. B., and Sullins, W. R. *Reexamining Community Services in the Community College: Toward Consensus and Commitment.* Topical Paper No. 76. Los Angeles: ERIC Clearinghouse for Junior Colleges and the National Council on Community Services and Continuing Education, 1982. 92 pp. (ED 220 138)

Beachler, J. A. "The Community Education Project: Pittsburgh, Pennsylvania." Paper presented at the annual conference of the National Council on Community Services and Continuing Education, Seattle, Oct. 1981. 38 pp. (ED 219 095)

Beachler, J. A. "Developing a Profile of the Continuing Education/Community Services Marketplace." Paper presented at the annual conference of the National Council on Community Services and Continuing Education, Detroit, Oct. 1982. 66 pp. (ED 226 766)

The Black Advisory Committee of Valencia Community College—Guidelines. Orlando, Fla.: Valencia Community College, 1980. 11 pp. (ED 229 059)

Brawer, F. B., and Gates, A. *Advisory Committees to the Humanities: A Handbook.* Topical Paper No. 74. Los Angeles: ERIC Clearinghouse for Junior Colleges, 1981. 29 pp. (ED 210 066)

Butler, D. G. *The Learning Community: An Examination of the Educational Interests and Future Educational Plans of the Community — Coast Community Colleges Community Telephone Survey, 1980.* Report No. 6. Costa Mesa, Calif.: Coast Community College District, 1981a. 19 pp. (ED 215 734)

Butler, D. G. *Purposes and Priorities: An Analysis of Community Attitudes Towards the Missions of the Community Colleges — Coast Community College Community Telephone Survey, 1980.* Report No. 5. Costa Mesa, Calif.: Coast Community College District, 1981b. 40 pp. (ED 215 733)

Citizens' Humanities Advisory Committee: Board Docket Items Establishing Committee and Minutes. San Diego: San Diego Community College District, 1983. 45 pp. (ED 226 793)

Clegg, M., and Tippett, C. *Caldwell Community College and Technical Institute Watauga Division Needs Assessment Survey.* Lenior, N.C.: Caldwell Community College and Technical Institute, 1982. 65 pp. (ED 224 529)

Demaris, C. "An Approach to Marketing Vocational Programs." Unpublished paper, 1980. 9 pp. (ED 211 149)

Dennis-Rounds, J. *Community Needs Assessment, Spring 1982.* Norwalk, Calif.: Office of Institutional Research, Cerritos College, 1983. 95 pp. (ED 226 794)

Gleazer, E. J., Jr. *The Community College: Values, Vision, and Vitality.* Washington, D.C.: American Association of Community and Junior Colleges, 1980. 197 pp. (ED 187 364; available in microfiche only)

Gollattscheck, J. F. "Community-Based Education: A New Direction for Community Colleges." In H. M. Jellison (Ed.), *Interface in Retrospect, 1978–1980.* Washington, D.C.: American Association of Community and Junior Colleges and the National Center for Community Education, 1980. 44 pp. (ED 200 289)

Groff, W. H. "Assisting a College's Service Area in the Transition to the New Technology Society Through Strategic Planning and Management." Unpublished paper, 1983. 40 pp. (ED 231 453)

HRD Yesterday and Today: A Statistical and Descriptive Study of the Human Resources Development Program Operated under the North Carolina Department of Community Colleges from 1973– 1982 — Final Report. Chapel Hill, N.C.: MDC, Inc., 1982. 262 pp. (ED 217 942)

Hagerstown Junior College Advisory Committee Handbook. Hagerstown, Md.: Hagerstown Junior College, 1982. 10 pp. (ED 215 746)

Hakanson, J. W. "Community Development — Who Benefits?" Paper presented at the annual conference of the National Council on Community Services and Continuing Education, Danvers, Mass., Oct. 1980. 8 pp. (ED 203 965)

Hastings, C. R. *Community Survey, June 1982.* Waco, Tex.: McLennan Community College, 1982. 107 pp. (ED 226 787)

Hopson, C. S., Montgomery, M. D., Aspiazu, G., and Lagasse, E. M. "The Needs Assessment as a Planning Tool for the 1980s." Paper presented at the annual convention of the American Association of Community and Junior Colleges, New Orleans, April 1983. 31 pp. (ED 231 433)

Implementation of the Budget Act Language to Reduce State Apportionments to Community College Districts by $30 Million: A Report to the Legislature in Response to the 1982–1983 Budget Act. Sacramento: California Postsecondary Education Commission, 1982. 50 pp. (ED 226 780)

An Introduction to Community Education for Wisconsin. Bulletin No. 8010. Madison: Wisconsin State Department of Public Instruction, 1980. 23 pp. (ED 220 170)

Ireland, J., and Gegna, M. *The Future Management, Funding, and Scope of Community Services Education Within the Los Angeles Community College District.* Los Angeles: Los Angeles Community College District, 1983. 97 pp. (ED 229 071)

Jellison, H. M. (Ed.). *Interface Through Cooperative Agreements: Eleven Examples of How It Can Work.* Washington, D.C.: American Association of Community and Junior Colleges and the National Center for Community Education, 1981. 6 pp. (ED 206 366; available in microfiche only)

Lau, P. *Pasadena Area Community College District Community Needs Assessment Study — Final Report.* Pasadena, Calif.: Pasadena Area Community College, 1982. 43 pp. (ED 244 543)

Lieberman, J. E. "Educational Alternatives for a Changing Society: Teaching and Reaching the Community." Paper presented at the "Educational Alternatives for a Changing Society" conference, Miami, Florida, January 27–30, 1981. 13 pp. (ED 198 862)

McQuay, P. L., and Watters, E. A. *Advisory Councils: Role, Function, Status, Responsibility, and Operation — Position Paper.* Williamsport, Pa.: Williamsport Area Community College, 1980. 10 pp. (ED 197 788)

Mahoney, J. R. *Community College Centers for Contracted Programs: A Sequel to Shoulders to the Wheel.* Washington, D.C.: American Association of Community and Junior Colleges, 1982. 77 pp. (ED 229 061; available in microfiche only)

Moore, C. "An Assessment of the Attitudes and Program Needs of Commercial, Industrial, and Service Agencies from the Service Area of Washington Community College." Unpublished doctoral dissertation, Nova University, 1980. 121 pp. (ED 198 889)

Moore, G. R. "Short-Term Training—Where the Action Is!" Unpublished paper, 1982. 9 pp. (ED 226 789)

Muraski, E. J. *A Needs Assessment to Determine Employment Needs in Monroe County, Florida.* Key West: Florida Keys Community College and Monroe County School District, 1982. 71 pp. (ED 223 272)

Needham, R. L. *Patrick Henry Community College Needs Assessment: Comprehensive Report.* Greensboro: University of North Carolina; Martinsville, Va.: Patrick Henry Community College, 1982. 82 pp. (ED 220 145)

Reading Area Community College Needs Assessment Telephone Survey. Reading, Pa.: Reading Area Community College, 1981. 81 pp. (ED 225 608)

Rosberg, W. H. "An Examination of the Perceived Educational Needs of a Sample Population of the Service Area of Kirkwood Community College." Unpublished doctoral dissertation, Nova University, 1981. 89 pp. (ED 207 642)

Ryan, J., and Juba, S. *A Survey of Citizens' Views About Brookdale Community College.* Stony Brook, N.Y.: Brookdale International Institute, 1982. 47 pp. (ED 224 514)

Simpson, W. M. "The Small/Rural Community College's Role in Enhancing the Fine Arts." Paper presented at the annual convention of the American Association of Community and Junior Colleges, St. Louis, April 1982. 13 pp. (ED 215 748)

Stoehr, K. W., and Banerdt, J. *Walworth County Employer Needs Assessment Study.* Kenosha, Wis.: Gateway Technical Institute, 1983. 43 pp. (ED 229 097)

A Survey of the Attitudes of Adults Toward Continuing Education: Report of Findings — Final Report. New York: Kane, Parsons and Associates, 1980. 114 pp. (ED 212 328)

Taxation and Community Services: A Public Opinion Survey of Macomb County Residents. Warren, Mich.: Macomb County Community College, 1982. 48 pp. (ED 217 950)

User's Guide to Educational Marketing: A Practical Approach for Responding to Community Needs. Portland, Ore.: Portland Community College, 1981. 56 pp. (ED 206 364)

Waddell, T. K., and Hunt, D. A. *Needs Assessment for the Cochise County Community College District — Phase 1 Report.* Douglas, Ariz.: Cochise College, 1982. 105 pp. (ED 223 298)

Jim Palmer is the user services librarian at the ERIC Clearinghouse for Junior Colleges, University of California, Los Angeles.

Index